T0270395

It Really Is Just Good Business

I'm a massive fan of Schumacher's "Small is Beautiful" and the values he ascribes to are reflected in this beautiful, little book. *It Really Is Just Good Business* is a faced-paced, easy to read business book. The stand-out benefit for me is the wonderfully practical and yet always challenging style of the author. She won't let you off the hook!

Small and micro-business owners hate being patronised by so-called experts, but they will love going on this journey of improvement as a responsible business because the author has decades of real-life experience running her own small businesses. Her practical approach shines through.

If you want to be challenged and to improve, you and your business will love this book.

Tony Robinson OBE, Micro Business Champion and Speaker, author of *The Happipreneur* and *Freedom from Bosses Forever*

Jill Poet has performed a great service to those seeking how to succeed in business. With wisdom, Jill shares her almost 50 years of experience running her own business or working for micro and small businesses in a practical way. She lays out concrete evidence that being ethical and responsible as a business is not a cost. It brings in more profits. You will be able to immediately see how you can bring and promote responsibility in your business by implementing her advice. Jill also possesses the ability to deliver a clear road map that will enable you to effectively communicate your ethics to the world and get precise results over and over again. Follow her advice inside *It Really Is Just Good Business,* and you'll discover a whole new level of financial and ethical success.

Mitali Deypurkaystha, Founder of The Vegan Publisher, author of international bestseller *The Freedom Master Plan*

I loved Jill's book – hugely readable, highly relatable. I particularly like all the practical suggestions including those to give back to the community. The more businesses do this, even just a little, the more we can really make a change. Recommend a read for anyone who wants to run a business – but responsibly.

Jan Cavelle, author of *Scale for Success*

It Really Is Just Good Business is a great read for any business no matter what the size, it makes you look at your business in different ways. Gives you encouragement that you can make a difference one small step at a time.

Janet Jack, CEO of the Institute of Accountants and Bookkeepers, and the International Association of Accounting Professionals

There is no doubt that culture in business is changing. Jill is the ultimate expert in the UK on this transition and how it is being driven forward by passionate small business owners. In *It Really Is Just Good Business,* Jill gives a personable, easy to read account of how business culture is evolving and why, using plenty of real-life examples.

Mike Jennings, Chairman of the Jennings Group of Companies, author of *Valuable: How a Values Enabled Culture Can Inspire You to Sustainable Profit*

It is becoming clearer by the year that businesses that purely exist for profit alone are not the future. It is essential for the future of humanity that eventually all businesses have a social and environmental purpose. It is the myriad of small businesses that have led the way on being a force for good, and Jill has been a pioneer of the movement through the Organisation for Responsible Businesses. Her book, *It Really Is Just Good Business*, in a common-sense style, shows the way that you as a small business can make a difference – the practical examples, business wisdom and case studies make this essential reading for the successful small businesses of the future.

Paul Hargreaves, CEO of Cotswold Fayre & Flourish, B Corp Ambassador, author of *Forces for Good* and *The Fourth Bottom Line*

Adnams has been pursuing a responsible business strategy for many years. This is led through its purpose and driven by its values. This approach is often seen as the domain of large corporates, and nothing could be further from the truth. Jill brings to life the role of the small and medium sized businesses, highlights opportunities and makes an important contribution to the wider debate.

Dr Andy Wood OBE DL, CEO of Adnams Plc, ex Professor of Corporate Leadership at University of East Anglia, co-author of *Creating a Lean and Green Business System*

I commend *It Really Is Just Good Business* not just to small businesses but also to senior corporate managers, politicians and policy makers, business consultants and advisers, students and educators — in fact, anyone interested in saving the planet for future generations. Not only is it comprehensive and clearly written, it is also packed with real-life cases and written from experience by someone who is passionate about the topic. Perhaps of more importance still, it is hard-hitting and makes the point that we are never too small to make a difference.

Professor David A. Kirby, BA, PhD, author of *Entrepreneurship*, co-author of *Small Firms and Economic Development in Developed and Transition Economies,* and co-founder of Harmonious Entrepreneurship Society

Business has spent two centuries creating pollution, climate change, biodiversity loss and resource depletion. We now have 50 years to use the tools of business to put things right. This welcome and exciting book recruits small businesses to that task - without losing sight of their primary function of financial success.

Tom Levitt, Centre for Responsible Business Advisory Board Member, author of *Welcome to GoodCo, The Company Citizen, The Courage to Meddle*

Corporate social responsibility (CSR) and good corporate citizenship are no longer the preserve of big business! Shining a light on the 'what' and the 'how' small businesses navigate the complexities of CSR and understand its relevance to them is long overdue. Jill's excellent book does this. It provides insights, examples and a blueprint for the 5 million small businesses which constitute 99% of all private businesses in the UK to help understand how CSR might help them in all facets of their business, become more sustainable (in terms of the planet and their own longer-term survival), create and deliver their own CSR programmes and, thereby, become better corporate citizens. I commend this excellent and practical book to all businesses from the smallest to the largest.

Rob Challis, Founder and CEO of Tangent Synergy Limited, Chairman of Trekstock and Success Club CIO charities

As an author and ESG advisor myself, I can wholeheartedly recommend *It Really Is Just Good Business* as an informative and worthwhile read. Jill's informal, conversational style makes her content memorable and easy to digest. Her relevant quotes are well placed. Unlike other standards, Jill's references to business continuity planning are critically important when we consider the pandemic impacts and that most start-ups and early-stage businesses fail to reach five years old. Applying this book to your business can open opportunities and tenders to major accounts with large supply chains. That's proof values sustain value.

Clive Bonny, Director of Strategic Management Services and PassivPod, co-author of *Business Ethics*, author of *Salesperson's Pocketbook*

It Really Is Just Good Business

...the art of operating a responsible, ethical, AND profitable small business

It Really Is Just Good Business

...the art of operating a responsible, ethical, AND profitable small business

Jill Poet

BUSINESS
BOOKS

Winchester, UK
Washington, USA

JOHN HUNT PUBLISHING

First published by Business Books, 2023
Business Books is an imprint of John Hunt Publishing Ltd., No. 3 East St., Alresford,
Hampshire SO24 9EE, UK
office@jhpbooks.com
www.johnhuntpublishing.com
www.johnhuntpublishing.com/business-books

For distributor details and how to order please visit the 'Ordering' section on our website.

Text copyright: Jill Poet 2022

ISBN: 978 1 80341 194 1
978 1 80341 195 8 (ebook)
Library of Congress Control Number: 2022940001

A CIP catalogue record for this book is available from the British Library.

Design: Lapiz Digital Services

UK: Printed and bound by CPI Group (UK) Ltd, Croydon, CR0 4YY
Printed in North America by CPI GPS partners

We operate a distinctive and ethical publishing philosophy in
all areas of our business, from our global network of authors to
production and worldwide distribution.

Contents

Dedication

To my business partner, my husband, my soulmate.
This book is dedicated to you.
Thank you, Mike. Without your unconditional love and
support this book would never have been written.

Acknowledgements

This book is a consequence of the many years of visioning, launching and managing the Organisation for Responsible Businesses and then committing the experiences and knowledge accumulated during that time to paper. Therefore, I would like to thank everyone who has played a part in that journey, starting with my husband and fellow director who has supported me throughout all the twists and turns of this great adventure - including reading many drafts of this book.

An enormous thank you to all our wonderful ORB members who have been so loyal in their support, many of whom are featured in this book.

Thank you to Dr Beatriz Acevedo, Senior Lecturer in Sustainability at Anglia Ruskin University who worked with us to develop the Responsible Business Standard; Rob Challis, an expert in CSR, who loved what we were doing and generously gave his time to deliver training to prospective RBS auditors; Rob Hines, Adrian Ashton, Clive Bonny and Sadie Restorick who were all on those early courses and are now on ORB's Advisory Board.

A special thank you to Kirsten Woodgate who is not only ORB's social media guru and a new director, but a true friend who has always been there to support and encourage me when the going got tough.

A huge thank you to Tony Robinson OBE. His enthusiasm and support is quite overwhelming. I love having Tony on both the Advisory Board and as a director as he ensures our passion for micro businesses is at the fore of everything we do.

Thank you to Ruairi Devlin for encouraging us to open membership of ORB in Ireland.

Thank you to everyone who took the time to read this book and provide feedback and reviews, especially as they read it before it was much improved by the editing process. I hope you enjoy reading the upgraded version, for which I thank Sharon Callcutt who appeared in my life as if by magic at just the right time to take on that editing role.

Thank you to everyone on our Advisory Board, new Board of Directors and the new Member Council. Thank you for personally supporting me and continuing to support ORB.

And a big thank-you to so many other people who have supported me at various stages on this journey. My apologies for not mentioning you all by name, but you know who you are, and I will be forever grateful.

And of course, a big thank-you to the team at John Hunt Publishing, especially Frank Smecker for supporting the editorial and production process, and Gavin Davies, who encouraged me to submit my manuscript, supported the application and guided me through the marketing process. Thank you all for having faith in me.

Introduction

A Different Way Of Doing Business

This book introduces a different way of doing business – a better way! A way that combines profitability with embedded ethics and values.

In today's society, your customers increasingly want more than good products and services. They want to know that your company cares about people which in turn means caring about the environment. It may not be the primary consideration for everyone, but it can certainly be the deciding factor in most cases. So, naturally, we will discuss this in more detail in the following chapters.

But responsible business *also* means having appropriate systems to ensure operational efficiency, reduce risk, and meet and exceed legislation. By adopting this pragmatic, broad-based, holistic approach to responsible business, your company will flourish and be more profitable and sustainable for the longer term.

But this book is not about that lofty aspiration of perfection; it aims to provide a realistic strategy that enables businesses to strive for continual improvement. It's an approach that cherishes small steps and the power of the journey.

As the saying goes:

'Inch by inch is a cinch; mile by mile is a trial.'

Who Is This Book For?

- Budding entrepreneurs and start-ups
- Sole proprietors and freelancers
- Micro and small business owners
- Company directors
- Social entrepreneurs
- Charity CEOs
- Senior managers
- Front line managers
- HR personnel
- Marketing professionals
- Business students
- Business advisors and consultants
- CSR and sustainability professionals
- Academics

Our focus is on **micro and small businesses,** but the same principles can be readily applied to corporate giants.

Getting Maximum Benefit From This Book

This book isn't a novel. There isn't a plot that you need to follow. It is merely a collection of my thoughts and experiences miraculously spilt onto paper. Okay. That is a slight exaggeration. I wish it had been that easy. But the point is, you do not need to read this book from cover to cover. I implore you to begin by reading Chapter 1, but otherwise, feel free to dip in and out as you wish. There will be aspects that you might want to miss altogether. For example, there is quite an extensive section on social enterprise that you may feel is just not for you. However, there is often a sting in the tail that relates to just how important micro and small businesses are. So, even if a chapter or section is not your top priority, please check it out at some point.

A point to note is that the intention of this book is not to tell you what to do. Instead, it encourages you to consider what is important to you and how it relates to your business. I don't adopt a one-size fits all approach. Micro and small businesses are, by their very nature, so richly diverse. We must cherish that diversity, but we can all be better. We can all improve. And starting with baby steps can sometimes be the best way to start.

Why Me?

When running a small business, I've been there, done that, got the t-shirt, and starred in the video. I know the challenges. I know how tough it is to run a small business.

My professional background is management accountancy. I don't have a sustainability degree. I don't come from a third-sector background. But for nearly 50 years, I have been running my own business or working for micro and small businesses from several different sectors.

My passion is micro and small businesses. But equally, my passion is to encourage those businesses to consider how they can positively impact society and how, by doing so, they will be more profitable.

My partner and now husband, Mike Wilson, and I launched the Organisation for Responsible Businesses (ORB) in 2010 with a mission to:

'Change the world – one small business at a time.'

But despite that somewhat grandiose mission statement, I have a very pragmatic approach to what we call 'responsible business'.

In 2011, we also launched the Responsible Business Standard, a comprehensive, robust, evidence-based certification specifically designed for small businesses and validated by Anglia Ruskin University.

To reiterate our philosophy, ethical and responsible business can be the most profitable and sustainable. In other words, I will be showing you that:

* * *

DOING GOOD IS GOOD FOR BUSINESS

Chapter 1 It's All About You

Now I promise you; this is NOT a soft, fluffy, wishy-washy book. Instead, this is a hard-core business manual – or at least a first-stage introduction. But this chapter has an emotional depth that is essential to explore before we move on.

Feel free to dip in and out of other chapters and read them in any order, but please give this chapter sufficient thought before you move on to the next one.

I would like you to start with a moment of self-reflection. And to do this properly, once you have read the following, I would like you to close your eyes and think deeply about the questions for at least a minute. Don't set a timer because if you are deep in thought, that would be an unnecessary interruption, but a minute with your eyes closed can seem a surprisingly long time. So, try it with a timer first.

You will need to reflect on when you started your business, if you are already operational, and then think about where you are now. If you are just getting started, then this is about intent. Ask yourself these questions:

- What did I want to achieve when I started this business? What was the purpose?
- Was that purpose just making a profit, or was it something more than that?
- Am I still guided by that purpose or has my purpose changed?
- If the purpose has changed, is that for the better or not?
- What are my values and ethics?
- Are they aligned with my business?

- Do my employees, customers, and suppliers know my values?
- Do my employees, customers, and suppliers know the company's values?
- What do people say about me and my business when I am not in the room?
- Will I be proud of my company's legacy?
- Will my children and other family members be proud of the business I have created?
- Does running my business make me feel happy and fulfilled?

One of the words I will frequently use in this book is **authenticity.** Being authentic ensures actions are based on embedded core values instead of a box-ticking exercise akin to greenwashing.

But whatever stage you are at now, if you genuinely want to operate an ethical and responsible business and care about people and the environment, you can quickly start taking the practical steps I'll discuss in the following chapters.

But let me be frank: if you are only interested in making a profit and other people do not matter to you, this book is not for you.

As I have already stressed, ethical and responsible business can be the most profitable and sustainable. Yet if you are not authentic in your thoughts and actions, you will be caught out pretty quickly. If profit is your only real motivation, all I will say is that *"money cannot buy you happiness!"*

Assuming you are still with me, let's move on…

Stop Compartmentalising!

At this stage, many of you may have realised that although you do have a strong personal moral code, you perhaps act slightly differently when in 'business mode'. That is probably due to compartmentalisation.

As a generalisation, men are more prone to this than women. That isn't a sexist slur: I am a firm believer in equality but let's be honest – men and women are different. Our brains work in different ways. Men typically have a stronger motor function and spatial recognition than women – hence the inevitable women-driver jokes! But women are more adept at logical reasoning and intuition. It's just the way our brains tend to be hard-wired. Men tend to act without considering the broader logical, social or emotional impacts. So, in the business environment, action is generally determined by maximising profit without considering the wider consequences of those actions.

Moving away from male/female differences, how many people do you know who are amiable as individuals but perhaps not so pleasant in the workplace? Could that be you?

Why Ethics Alone Is Not Enough

Perhaps you already think you are a very ethical person operating a very ethical business. But that just might not be enough. Sometimes, adopting that stance is more akin to the 'do no harm' approach than proactively doing good!

Let's dig a little deeper...

How do you define ethics? Quite simply, you can't! No benchmark or defining line in the sand can dictate what is and isn't ethical.

Let's start by looking at definitions in the Concise Oxford Dictionary:

Ethical: *'relating to morals.'*

Morals: *'conforming to accepted standards of human behaviour.'*

Oh, my goodness! How in the world do we define 'accepted standards'? These will differ in every country, every religion, and every era in our rich history. What you might consider an accepted standard of human behaviour may be quite different from the views of your next-door neighbour; and even your life partner. And if you have children, their perception of acceptable standards of behaviour is no doubt vastly different!

So, who is right? Who is wrong?

Let's put this in the perspective of the fashion industry.

You are undoubtedly aware of sweat-shop labour and the horrendous factory conditions in developing countries. You may remember the Bangladesh factory collapse. Or perhaps you have heard about the number of workers in cotton fields poisoned by heavy use of pesticides without being given appropriate protective clothing or are appalled by the cruelty of child labour?

I am sure you would not treat your employees in such a manner. I am sure that this isn't something you would condone. These practices are unethical, aren't they? But they are nonetheless commonplace practices in the supply chain in the fashion industry. Why? Because in the Western world, we have a seemingly insatiable desire for cheap clothing! Yes, we (and I include myself in this because I don't hold myself out as a paragon of virtue) are quite possibly wearing clothes made by someone who has suffered appallingly in the process of manufacturing them.

Sorry, that is not a pleasant thought – but perhaps a necessary one.

So, does that make us bad, unethical people? No, I don't think so. However, giving more thought to our choices can often be a daunting challenge – although perhaps we might give our clothing purchases a bit more consideration in the future.

The point is that YOU must make your own decision about what ethical means to you. Draw your line in the sand. But once you have done that, stand by it; and continually strive to improve. Don't ever let the line slip back. We cannot be perfect, and we cannot change the world overnight, but we can take baby steps every day that can start to make a difference. Ultimately, we must hold ourselves to account and think about the broader picture of our actions.

Taking it a step further...

A good example is membership of a professional body. Members of such organisations are invariably required to adhere to a Professional Code of Ethics. Looking at the ACCA as an example, the organisation has fully integrated the International Code of Ethics for Professional Accountants into their specific Code of Ethics, detailed in a comprehensive 331-page document. The fundamental principles of the code are:

- Integrity
- Objectivity
- Professional Competence and Due Care

- Confidentiality
- Professional Behaviour

Although supplementary information about sustainability is on the ACCA website, nothing about making a positive societal impact is included in the main Code of Ethics.

The following case study illustrates why 'being an ethical business' is just not enough.

CASE STUDY

At the Organisation for Responsible Businesses, we always have a Zoom meeting with the business owner or a senior representative before we approve the membership to ensure the organisation fits the essence of the responsible business movement. We do not expect perfection, but a commitment to considering people and the planet alongside profit is essential, even if that commitment is at a comparatively early stage of implementation.

Vera, not her real name, was a very pleasant lady interested in becoming a member of ORB. During our conversation, she explained that she had faced challenging times over recent years and was in the process of rebuilding her accountancy practice. She was working with small traders and wanted to attract the bigger clients she had worked with in a previous company and, to do so, was building a new team.

We chatted for some time. But at no point did Vera talk about supporting her local community or a commitment to reducing environmental impacts. When I asked the question, she stressed that her focus was rebuilding the business; she had been very altruistic in the past but could not be so now. She did not feel she was 'any less environmentally friendly than most people'!

I attempted to elucidate the 'doing good is good for business' message and that proactively embracing responsible business practices would support her attempts at rebuilding her business, but my explanations fell on deaf ears.

When I gently explained that, unfortunately, she did not fit the membership profile, she was slightly surprised and repeatedly stressed that she operated a very ethical business.

I had no doubt that Vera did indeed run an ethical business based on honesty, integrity, professionalism and confidentiality, characteristics one would certainly expect from an accountant.

But in that instance, ethics alone certainly was not enough!

* * *

If you are that ethical businessperson, we hope reading this book will help elevate your business to another level and that soon you will be reaping the emotional, spiritual and financial rewards of being a more proactive ethical business, one that embraces a purpose-driven approach to making a positive contribution to society.

The world is not perfect, but we can make a difference, however small our business is. After all, over 5 million businesses in the

UK are micro-businesses (employing 0–9 people), accounting for 33 per cent of private sector employment and 18 per cent of turnover.

Our actions may seem insignificant but collectively can make a massive change for the better.

'Be the change that you wish to see in the world.'
Mahatma Gandhi

Let's Raise a Glass to ASTI
I'm rather partial to a glass of fizz, albeit not necessarily Asti!

But this section is about a different sort of ASTI. And as you read this book, especially if you are already feeling a little daunted, ASTI should always be at the forefront of your thoughts.

A APPROPRIATE

S SIZE

T TYPE

I IMPACT

ASTI, Appropriate to the Size, Type and Impact of your business, is the basis of our approach to responsible business at ORB.

As I explained, I have nearly 50 years of experience working with small businesses, but my goodness, they vary so much. Not just in sector and size, but in so many other elements that are pretty unique to each specific business.

So, let's put responsible business in perspective: there is no one-size-fits-all benchmark.

Certain aspects in this book may not apply to you at all, such as the workplace section – although do check out the introduction to that section because it may be worth you reading it for a variety of reasons.

My intent, therefore, is not to tell you to do this or do that but to encourage you to think about how a specific topic relates to your business and, if it is relevant, to ask yourself if you are doing as well as you should do in that area, could you improve, and what steps might you take in that process.

The answers are relevant to your specific business. You have the answers – not us!

* * *

But did I also tell you that DOING GOOD IS GOOD FOR BUSINESS!

Chapter 2 What's in It For Me?

We've seen one catastrophic business scandal after another in a comparatively short space of time, including the near collapse of the banking system, the ongoing Volkswagen emissions debacle, Facebook's data breaches, the cladding crisis that followed the Grenfell Tower fire, and so many more; all caused because companies, or individuals in those companies, put profit before people: before any sense of responsible business conduct.

But with each new scandal, reputations have plummeted, and millions of pounds have been wiped off share values.

Although your business is probably not a PLC, reputational damage can similarly affect small businesses. In today's social-media-driven world, there is just no escape from public opinion and scrutiny.

Quite simply, the rules of business have changed. Greed has been the defining god of the business world for far too long: now, allegiance to the creed of money alone will ultimately result in failure. In this era of fast-paced social media, reputations can be irrevocably damaged almost overnight. And small businesses are certainly not immune from the phenomena.

We must make a choice. We either decide to continue as we are, ignoring any bad practices or just making sure we don't get caught. Or we can strive to be better.

One of our best-known entrepreneurs certainly appreciates that the business world has changed and must continue to change; if we want to be successful, we need to do things differently. As

Richard Branson said in his book *Screw Business as Usual*, first published in 2011:

> Never has there been a more exciting time for all of us to explore this great next frontier where the boundaries between work and purpose are merging into one, where doing good, really is good for business.

But I am a realist. As mentioned, I have a lifetime of experience in the small business world. I know only too well that however well-intentioned a business owner may be, the day-to-day challenges of running a business will likely take precedence over changing the status quo unless the ever-present 'What's in it for me' question can be satisfactorily answered.

In other words, how can a company benefit by heeding the suggestions in this book?

As we work through the chapters, I will be digging down in more detail with the benefits in each section: with the cause and effect. This chapter only intends to give a quick overarching view of the potential benefits.

Increased Reputation

In today's social-media-driven society, every business comes under scrutiny, and word-of-mouth referrals now mean much more than conversations between friends, family and neighbours. Similarly, most businesses have websites and their own social media channels that can broadcast to hundreds if not thousands of potential customers.

But any savvy marketer will explain that posts or information on websites about the good things you are doing, such as a commitment to net zero; raising funds for a local charity; positive reviews about superb service; employees extolling the virtues of a great company vibe; are all gold dust in terms of increasing reputation – providing they are authentic, of course!

Recent research shows that 84 per cent of marketers believe building trust will be the primary focus of future marketing campaigns. Why? Because people are fed up with being ripped off and mistreated by businesses that cause societal problems because they only care about making a profit.

Building trust as a socially responsible company is the best way to build your reputation. And a good reputation is one of your company's most important assets.

Inspiring Innovation

When business leaders make a commitment to operating ethically and responsibly, they should thoroughly review their business to ensure all aspects of operations fit company values. This fresh viewpoint often opens doors to a different way of doing business. Different questions will be asked. The status quo is disrupted. And innovation usually follows, whether that is simply finding ways of recycling waste that has previously gone to landfill, sourcing new products that meet today's ethical trends or adopting hybrid working practices.

New Business Opportunities

There are also a growing number of innovative businesses in all sectors that have launched new products or services based on a desire to create social value over and above a desire to make a profit. However, those aspirations do not need to be mutually exclusive.

Additionally, many existing businesses will adapt and, because small businesses are generally very nimble, will do this quickly. This may be by adding to their current products or services, niching, or completely pivoting the business model.

Excellent Marketing Opportunities

As stated in the reputation section, social media posts and blogs about the good things you are doing and the positive difference you make are gold dust.

Marketers typically recommend the 80/20 rule where only 20 per cent of your social media should be directly about your business and self-promotional content, and the other 80 per cent should be more general, engaging information. It is not a rule fixed in stone and will vary according to the nature of the business, but the essence of the rule is that people don't like to be bombarded with sales messages. Sharing content about supporting a local charity, or posts on World Mental Health Day about how you support your employees' mental wellbeing, are just two examples of posts that are likely to be well received by your audience and still shine a light on your company but are not salesy.

Certain businesses take the view that they do not want to publicise their charitable activities, but we would urge them to reconsider for two reasons:

1. People genuinely like to hear these stories – providing they are authentic!
2. The more businesses talk about their actions to contribute positively to society, the more it will become the norm.

Winning Contracts

This is such a crucial element that we shall explore it in depth at a later stage but suffice to say, any company intending to bid for private or public sector contracts may be required to identify the social value they bring to a contract.

Attract and Retain the Best People

In more recent years, an ever-increasing number of the brightest employees want more than just a good salary package; they want to work for a company that feeds their values.

As generation Z enters the workplace, loosely young people born between 1995 and 2010, they will expect their employers to demonstrate a commitment to a broad range of societal challenges such as climate change, equality and diversity, and poverty.

A study by WeSpire found that Gen-Z is:

> The first generation to prioritise purpose over salary. They read Mission Statements and Values documents to select where they work and want their employer's values to match their values. They expect consistency and authenticity and will call you out, often publicly, if they do not see it. They will leave companies they believe are hiding or putting too much spin on bad news, ignoring their negative environmental or social impacts, or that have toxic workplace cultures.

More bright young people are leaving behind corporate careers with good salaries and benefits and looking for a role that provides more purpose, often with a smaller business, social enterprise or charity, or even launching their own business.

CASE STUDY

As Kayleigh Nicolaou, who is typical of the generation known as millennials (born between 1980 and 1994), which already forms a high percentage of the workforce, explains:

When we set up Kakadu Creative, some of our friends thought we were mad.

Lee Skellett and I were both working for one of the biggest multi-national publishers in the world and had built up strong careers and healthy salaries to boot. We were comfortable, and we had a secure future ahead. So why give all that up and risk the uncertainty of starting your own agency?

But, whilst on the surface we looked like we had it all sewn up, in truth, we were unfulfilled. Working for a large-scale corporate business where revenue and profit were the number one point of conversation meant it was hard to see what positive impact we were having on the world around us. Especially when just getting a basic recycling system in place for the three-storey, 600+ employee office we worked in was a battle?

So, what was the alternative?

Well, after much deliberation, we decided enough was enough, and it was time we went our own way and set up an ethical and sustainable design agency. An agency that puts people and planet before profits, and an agency that helps to support other businesses with the same mission.

* * *

Increased Staff Engagement and Motivation

One of the best ways to empower employees is through effective delegation. Inviting employees to take on the mantle of social and environmental planning can be incredibly rewarding for all involved.

Extensive research shows that a sense of purpose is key to employee engagement. Similarly, as embedding responsible business practices help attract the best people, purpose also helps engage, motivate and retain existing staff.

Had Kayleigh and Lee been employed in a more purpose-driven business, perhaps they would have never left! I am sure they would have jumped at the opportunity to help the company develop an environmental programme.

Social and environmental considerations should be part of a strategy aligned with a company's purpose and values. The starting point should always be to consider any improvements to support the health and wellbeing of staff or any other internal issues that may need addressing.

Many large companies have CSR (Corporate Social Responsibility) departments with dedicated staff to implement social and environmental actions. Some of these departments do excellent work, but others are more than a little disappointing as they operate virtually autonomously. They do not engage staff and are more concerned with initiating outward-facing CSR projects that create impactful reading in End of Year Reports rather than focusing on the most meaningful options.

If responsible business is not genuinely embraced across all levels of an organisation, the CSR box might be ticked, but the organisation's culture is not being nurtured and could even be damaged if employees feel the company is not genuinely walking the talk.

Most of our case studies are positive, although some, such as the following example, are decidedly negative!

CASE STUDY

An example that hit the headlines in 2021 is BrewDog, a brewery based in Scotland but now with breweries and bars worldwide. BrewDog is growing internationally at a phenomenal rate and making impressive strides in environmental sustainability.

But...

As well as many similar statements on its website, BrewDog's highly detailed company accounts for the year ending 31 December 2020 state:

> BrewDog is built on a commitment to its crew. Our people are the beating heart of our business, they are the reason we exist and the thing we work hardest to protect and develop.

In February 2021, BrewDog qualified as a B Corp, something held aloft as confirmation that a company is meeting high standards of social and environmental performance. (B Corp is discussed in Chapter 4.) And yet, in June 2021, 61 former employees of BrewDog signed a lengthy open letter describing a toxic culture that left staff suffering from mental illness; continual PR campaigns based on lies, hypocrisy and deceit; and instructions to ignore health and safety guidelines. Perhaps the most chilling comment in the letter was:

> Being treated like a human being was sadly not always a given for those working at BrewDog.

Since the company launched in 2007, there have clearly been ongoing issues creating distress for many of its employees. But the disclosure of these issues has now publicly damaged the company's reputation.

* * *

In smaller businesses, employees are far more likely to be directly involved. Often, there will be individuals within a company who are keen to be charity or environmental champions, who are extremely happy to rally and engage with their peers to discuss priorities and recommend and implement strategies and activities as approved by the business owner/senior executives. Even if your company only has a few employees, you are probably immediately aware of who these people might be.

Encouraging employees to play an active role in the approach to community and environmental actions – not just getting involved in the 'doing' but also helping to develop appropriate strategies that fit the company's purpose and values – increases engagement and motivation. Of course, not every employee will get actively involved, but nonetheless, the culture across the whole company will be elevated.

Engaged employees are happy employees; happy employees create a motivated and productive workforce delivering superb results and increasing profits, which could be partially allocated to further workplace community, and environmental improvements, engaging the workforce further. As the diagram below shows, this delivers a virtuous circle of boosted profitability driven by increased employee motivation and engagement and enhanced opportunities for the company to deliver positive societal impacts.

Virtuous Circle of Employee Engagement

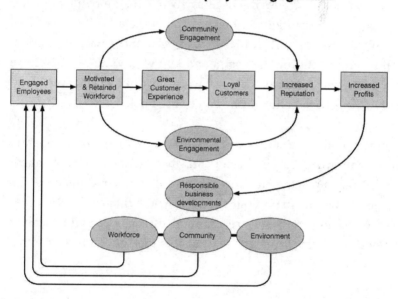

Mitigate Risks

Every company, whatever size and type, faces potential risks, which is why business continuity plans are essential.

We have already mentioned reputational risk at the beginning of this chapter which can be incredibly damaging. Other risks that can be mitigated by embracing responsible business practices are as follows – remembering that each of these also has the potential to damage reputation:

1. Compliance Risk

Business owners face an abundance of legislation they must comply with, and fines and penalties can be surprisingly large.

Small businesses with few employees find employment legislation, including health and safety requirements, can be particularly onerous. Developing a good workplace culture will reduce that risk, but having appropriate systems in place is essential. This does not necessarily mean employing or hiring expensive consultants to help you; there is a multitude of free advice and support available for micro and small businesses. But understanding the basics and knowing what resources are available is essential. This is covered further in Chapter 7 and the Resources section at the end of the book.

Most small businesses are subject to limited environmental legislation, but specific sectors may need to meet more stringent requirements. Do you know what applies to your business? Do you know how to find out? Did you know that certain breaches of environmental law are criminal offences carrying heavier fines that also leave the responsible person with a criminal conviction?

In 2020, the Environment Agency issued an increasing number of penalties, including the largest ever environmental offence in the UK: a £51.9 million enforcement undertaking levied on an airline which failed to meet its responsibilities under the EU Emissions Trading Scheme.

But smaller businesses are not immune from big fines:

A housing developer demolished a building in which protected soprano pipistrelle bats were roosting. The firm was fined £600,000 plus £30,000 costs and agreed to make a voluntary donation of £20,000 to the Bat Conservation Trust.

A scrap dealer was fined over £400,000 for running an illegal car breaker's yard.

However, in most instances, the Environment Agency will respond to breaches with a warning followed by a formal caution before legal action is taken. Nonetheless, this is never a good situation to find yourself in.

In Chapter 8, we will look at environmental legislation and best practice in more detail.

2. **Security and Fraud**
Data breaches, identity theft and payment fraud, are also areas of considerable risk for small businesses. Any of these issues can damage trust and reputation, and companies may also be financially liable for damages.

The best staff, appropriate employee training, and excellent business practices are essential. And yes, that is all part of being a responsible business.

3. **Competition Risk**
Virtually every business has competition in their industry which is a healthy situation for all concerned, especially customers.

Fortunately, micro-businesses in similar industries choose to work collaboratively, which is invariably a win-win. Nonetheless, it is essential to be aware of direct competition.

To maintain and grow your position in the relevant marketplace and stand out from the crowd, every business needs to continually reassess its performance and strategies. Are you constantly able to pivot and make continual improvements?

Embracing the principles of responsible business might be one of the most important aspects of improvement: if your competitors are evidencing their social and environmental credentials and you are not, and all else is comparable, where are your potential clients likely to place their custom?

Gaining New Skills

There are infinite ways in which small companies can support the local community, learning new skills along the way as well as a greater understanding of the broader issues in the local area.

Considering environmental improvements within the company will invariably involve discussion and research that results in a broader understanding of environmental issues that may impact our approach on a personal basis too.

These are just a few examples:

- Leadership skills
- Problem-solving
- Organisation and planning
- Communication and people skills
- Relationship building
- Mentoring skills and training others
- Teamwork
- Time management
- Effective reporting

- Raised confidence and self-esteem
- Physical skills such as decorating, gardening and developing wildlife habitats

and many, many more…

You'll Feel Good Too!

You should never underestimate this aspect. It could almost be the most important element for you. Operating a profitable and thriving business that contributes positively to society will help ensure your working life is enjoyable.

As an additional bonus, you will also be able to proudly tell your children and grandchildren what you are doing/what you have done in your working life to make this world a better place.

That will make them happy – and extra proud – too!

Chapter 3 No One Cares About That Stuff

Year on year, there is a huge increase in the value of the 'green' pound, the amount spent on ethical products and investments. According to the Co-op's Ethical Consumerism Report 2021, green spending surged in the UK by nearly a quarter in 2020 to £122bn, with £61bn spent on ethical products and services, including plant-based foods, second-hand clothes and furniture, greener gadgets, and a further £57bn of ethical savings and investments.

The report also confirmed that consumers' shopping habits were increasingly reflected in their concerns about the environment, social justice, and animal welfare, with shoppers boycotting brands where specific social or environmental concerns have been flagged. The report suggests that specifically boycotted businesses suffered a loss of almost £4bn in sales.

For years, when talking with small businesses about caring about people and the environment, one of the responses has invariably been:

'No one asks me about that stuff. No one cares.'

Of course, not everyone cares or can make decisions based on ethics, as cost is their priority. But unquestionably, and more so than ever, a high percentage of consumers do care.

But even the most assiduous of ethical shoppers are unlikely to directly ask a business owner about their values and priorities. Some will, but not many. That does not mean they will not look at your website for appropriate information, scour social media, or ask friends, family, or employees if they know any.

The point is, you must TELL people what your values are – and substantiate any statements you make. Because they will look, they will ask, and they will increasingly make decisions based on that information.

These considerations are even more critical if you sell B2B or to the public sector. To increase your chances of winning contracts, you must demonstrate social and environmental responsibility effectively and robustly.

I have already spoken about millennials, and the next generations about to enter the workplace, wanting to work for companies with demonstrable values that resonate with their own. And in the following chapters, there are sections on social value driving social and environmental change down the supply chain and also on marketing and how to authentically tell the story of the good things you are doing.

In the last 12 years, I have witnessed a considerable change in people's expectations. Without question, the desire to purchase goods and services from ethical and responsible companies is increasing exponentially. Have no doubt that if your competitors are evidencing they care about their employees and the local community and are committed to reducing their environmental impacts, and you are not, your business will soon start to decline!

Chapter 4 The Rules of Business Have Changed

The Purpose of Business

In 1962, Milton Friedman published the book *Capitalism and Freedom,* in which he says:

> There is one and only one social responsibility of business – to use its resources and engage in activities designed to increase its profits so long as it stays within the rules of the game, which is to say, engages in open and free competition without deception or fraud.

In 1970, Milton Friedman's essay 'The Social Responsibility of Business Is to Increase Its Profits' was published in the *New York Times*.

In 1976, Friedman was awarded the Nobel Prize for Economics. His sphere of influence continued to grow, resulting in his doctrines being adopted by most of the corporate world from the 1980s until recently.

In the business world, as a result of Friedman's work, there was an almost universal acceptance that a public company should maximise its profits and shareholder value above all else.

It was not until 2008, when the shock waves of the worldwide financial crisis impacted many companies' approach to more ethical leadership, that the principles of Corporate Social Responsibility (CSR) began to be more widely adopted, albeit primarily embraced as a means of reputational risk management.

The rules of the business world were slowly beginning to change. Even business schools acknowledged their historical roles in creating a business world unfit for purpose.

In 2009, I attended a graduation ceremony at the Essex Business School, University of Essex. Unexpectedly, the chancellor's speech was an apology: an apology that, for years, business schools across the UK, including the Essex Business School, had churned out graduates with an inappropriate approach to business.

Business schools had all delivered degree courses based on the edicts of Friedman, and it was that approach to business, the emphasis on maximising profits and shareholder value, that caused the financial crash.

The chancellor vowed this would change...and it has. The Essex MBA now states:

At Essex Business School, we are champions of responsible management and sustainable business. We use creativity and innovation to drive organisations forward and make them better places to do business.

Does Capitalism Work?
It would certainly seem that capitalism, as it exists today, is not working. Friedman's philosophy is still deeply embedded in the business psyche, and although there are signs of change, it can be difficult to gauge the authenticity of corporate messaging.

In a survey by the marketing and public relations firm Edelman in 2020, 57 per cent of people worldwide said that 'capitalism, as it exists today, does more harm than good in the world.'

Looking at the UK, without even considering the poverty in developing countries, it is immediately evident that many businesses, especially large corporates, are still prioritising the interests of shareholders above those of society, resulting in environmental damage and increased inequality.

Adam Smith is widely acknowledged as the father of capitalism and modern economics, publishing the renowned *The Wealth of Nations* in 1776. However, Adam Smith believed that capitalism would be a path to a better life across social classes.

He acknowledged that for most businesses, capitalism would be driven by a desire to make money rather than any altruistic intent. Nonetheless, he believed the core principles of fair pay, good working conditions, and good customer service were the most profitable ways to do business. Therefore any business striving to maximise profitability would play a significant role in a better society as an automatic result of commercial endeavours.

In Tom Levitt's book *Welcome to GoodCo: Using the Tools of Business to Create Public Good*, he confirms a belief that there is:

No serious alternative to capitalism as the predominant political force for the twenty-first century. Yet...

Capitalism is using up the world's non-renewable resources, hydrocarbons and minerals in a way that is irresponsible and will lead to shortages.

Capitalism is using up the world's renewable resources, too – clean water, timber and flora – faster than it replaces them. In particular, it's contributing to climate change...

Capitalism is creating capitalism in a way the market can't bear: 93 per cent of all new wealth created in the USA since the 2008 crash has gone to the richest 1 per cent of the population.

Capitalism appears to have abandoned many of the positive values it was credited with in times gone by, making them all subservient to the production of profit.

Sadly, Adam Smith underestimated one trait of human nature that would undermine the very essence of the capitalist system he envisaged: GREED.

The phrase 'money is the root of all evil' is often cited. But as Paul Hargreaves reminds us in his book *Forces for Good: Creating a Better World Through Purpose-Driven Business*, the full quote, which comes from the apostle Paul in his letter to his young disciple Timothy, is:

'The love of money is the root of all evil.'

Money in itself is not evil. Money is merely a means by which we can efficiently trade goods and services.

Money and the material things it enables us to purchase certainly cannot buy happiness. Of course, most people cannot be happy unless, at minimum, their basic needs such as food, water, shelter, clothing, warmth and sleep are met. We also need the emotional, physical and financial security that enables us to maintain a lifestyle that nurtures and protects our families and us. But to what degree do we need additional trappings of wealth?

In 2017, researchers from Purdue University in the United States identified interesting facts after analysing 1.7 million individuals over the age of 15 across 164 countries. In the UK, the research showed the income sweet spot was £68,000 per adult for overall life satisfaction. That is not to suggest that anyone with income below that level is necessarily unhappy, but that once the sweet spot was reached, 'further increases in income tended to be associated with reduced life satisfaction and a lower level of wellbeing.'

And yet culturally, the twin cycles of greed and consumerism combined with the increasing desire to showcase apparent success across social media channels is probably the most significant underlying cause of the current state of social inequalities and environmental degradation in the UK and worldwide. And business continues to greedily feed off that desire for more, more, more…!

Capitalism can only work effectively with government intervention to keep society functioning efficiently and equitably. In the simplest of terms, this includes legislation to protect all stakeholders of an organisation and taxation for the generation of funds for infrastructure and services to support society.

Legislation is often insufficient to prevent the malpractices of many organisations, and politics invariably influences levels and methods of taxation.

Statistics from the Census 2021 show that the wealthiest 10 per cent in Great Britain own around half of all wealth, primarily in private pensions and property. The top 1 per cent of households have a wealth of more than £3.6m each compared to the household wealth of £15,400 or less for the poorest 10 per cent. The bottom 50 per cent of the population holds only 9 per cent of the country's wealth. Among the poorest 10 per cent of households, almost half had more financial debt than they did assets.

Like Tom and Paul, Julian Richer is one of many proponents of a different type of capitalism which he calls Ethical Capitalism.

Julian established Richer Sounds in 1978. The company now turns over more than £200 million a year. He says:

> I am an absolute believer in capitalism. I am also deeply aware of its shortcomings.

In his book *The Ethical Capitalist: How to Make Business Work Better for Society*, there are several elements which I'll briefly encapsulate below. But the first clue is in the title – The Ethical Capitalist. In other words, the suggestion is that the solution lies with the individual instead of the system. In his book, these are the critical elements that Julian suggests businesses should implement:

- Value their employees, taking a 'people first' approach that manages and motivates staff. Julian believes this should include:

  ◦ paying the Living Wage
  ◦ ensuring the ratio of directors' pay to average employees' pay should not be excessive
  ◦ zero hours contracts should not be in place unless they are mutually beneficial for both employee and employer

- Always act with honesty and fairness with customers
- Treat suppliers fairly and with respect and always #Payin30Days

- Pay taxes properly rather than use avoidance schemes. (As we have seen, many big corporates operating in the UK pay minimal tax.)

Surprisingly, Julian has omitted to mention anything about caring about and reducing environmental impacts in his book. While I appreciate that he has focused very much on the 'people and society' aspect of good business, I would suggest that no one could genuinely be considered an ethical capitalist in the context of making business work better for society if environmental issues are not high on their agenda.

But if Julian, Paul and Tom et al. have outlined the problem and cited a change in how business operates as the solution, how do we ensure that those large corporations take heed and put these attributes into practice, particularly as it would seem this was what Adam Smith envisaged capitalism to be hundreds of years ago.

Is more government intervention required?

Will people-power force a change of behaviour?

Will a more enlightened younger generation, fearful of their future and refusing to work with unethical companies, be able to drive that change?

I suspect all these elements are important, but it will likely be a slow process. Much too slow!

Perhaps the best solution is a seismic move away from the world of big business and a greater focus on supporting, working with, and purchasing from responsible small businesses. But hey – as small business owners, we've got to quickly step up to the plate if we want that to happen.

But I'll reiterate: I believe micro and small businesses can cumulatively be a phenomenal power for good, much more so than their larger counterparts.

So please keep reading and ensure you are part of the responsible business movement that's good for business and society too!

The Better Business Act

The Companies Act 2006 still gives credence to shareholder supremacy as opposed to broader stakeholder interests. The Better Business Act (BBA) is a campaign initiated by B Lab UK and supported by hundreds of businesses, including the Organisation for Responsible Businesses. The campaign is asking the government to change section 172 of the Companies Act so that the interests of shareholders are aligned with the interests of our planet and society rather than taking precedence.

Currently, section 172 states:

172 Duty to promote the success of the company

1. A director of a company must act in the way he considers, in good faith, would be most likely to promote the success of the company for the benefit of its members as a whole, and in doing so have regard (amongst other matters) to —
   a. the likely consequences of any decision in the long term,
   b. the interests of the company's employees,
   c. the need to foster the company's business relationships with suppliers, customers and others,
   d. the impact of the company's operations on the community and the environment,
   e. the desirability of the company maintaining a reputation for high standards of business conduct, and
   f. the need to act fairly as between members of the company.

39

The changes requested by the BBA emphasise the *purpose of business* and would begin:

172 Duty to advance the purpose of the company

1. A director of a company must act in the way the director considers, in good faith, would be most likely to *advance the purpose of the company,* and in doing so have regard (amongst other matters) to the following considerations...

Additionally, the BBA suggests an amendment that would require all large companies to provide a strategic report for each financial year that details how the directors have advanced the purpose of the company and have had regard to the other matters in section 172(1) (a) to (f).

B Lab UK is a charity launched in 2015 to drive the development of the B Corp movement in the UK. There is more information about B Corp at the end of this section.

Corporate Social Responsibility (CSR)
Corporate Social Responsibility, or Corporate Responsibility, relates to an organisation's broader responsibilities to society. It *should* mean that a company actively aims to make a positive contribution to society and the environment rather than causing harm in accordance with the EU strategy for CSR published on 25th October 2011. This succinct definition of CSR states:

'the responsibility of enterprises for their impacts on society'

An extremely broad and holistic definition which also states that: 'respect for legislation is a requisite for meeting that responsibility' and that 'to fully meet their corporate social responsibility, enterprises should have in place a process to integrate social, environmental, ethical, human rights and consumer concerns into their business operations and core strategy in close collaboration with their stakeholders.'

Unfortunately, for many large companies for many years, CSR has been little more than a box-ticking exercise.

As we have already mentioned, CSR departments would typically be allocated budgets that would be used for 'CSR projects' to impress the outside world. Sadly, although the projects in themselves may have been effective, they were often totally unaligned with the general business behaviour of the company. But social media, combined with a more demanding and aware general public, and vociferous NGOs, ensures that it is no longer as easy for companies, however large and powerful, to play this game of smoke and mirrors.

Responsible Business

When we launched the Organisation for Responsible Businesses in 2010, the phrase responsible business wasn't commonly used. Naturally, because our focus was micro and small businesses, we wanted to avoid the term corporate. But with an acknowledgement of the inappropriate approach and, therefore, inadequacies of CSR, responsible business is now used more widely across the business landscape for organisations of all types and sizes.

But interestingly, as above, the term is also used in the EU's definition of CSR. Clearly, they copied our lead...!

In stark contrast to Milton Friedman's assertion that the responsibility of business is basically to make a profit, a responsible business takes a 'triple bottom line' approach, a term coined by John Elkington in 1994, meaning that it considers people and the environment in addition to profit in business operations. The term was intended as a challenge for business leaders to rethink capitalism. Ethical Capitalism, perhaps?

But in 2018, John Elkington 'took back' the term because although some companies genuinely adopted triple bottom line principles, it was mainly used by big corporates as an accounting tool as opposed to embedding a true culture in terms of doing business differently. In essence, most companies treated the concept the same way as CSR: lots of window dressing but minimal genuine culture change.

We have a slightly different definition of responsible business because, although our drive is absolutely to encourage businesses to adopt triple bottom line principles, an organisation of any type is only operating responsibly if it is also operating efficiently, with appropriate systems in place and also meeting legislation. In other words, while our purpose is to encourage businesses to make a positive impact on society, we must never forget that the basics of good business must be robustly maintained.

This is our definition:

> A responsible business operates efficiently and ethically; meets and exceeds legislation; and always considers its impact on people (the workforce, the community, society at large), and the environment.

The Responsible Business/Social Value course and certification options offered by ORB are aimed at driving the responsible business movement and encouraging business owners and senior executives to consider if they are really doing the best they can to make a positive impact on people and reduce the negative environmental impacts of their business, but meeting legislation and operating efficiently remain key elements of the certification requirements.

Membership of ORB is the first step for sole proprietors and small companies in becoming part of the responsible business movement, but as part of the application process, applicants are required to make the following pledge:

> We pledge to operate our business in an honest and ethical manner; to consider people and the environment when making business decisions; and endeavour to make a positive contribution to the local community and society at large.

When a company is accepted as a member of ORB, they have to complete a Members' Directory profile page, which not only tells consumers and organisations what goods and services they provide but what it is that makes their organisation a responsible business.

ORB has also developed the Responsible Business Standard, which is now offered as an online course and various certification options. At the highest level of certification, it is a very robust, evidence-based process and businesses with five or more employees are also required to have a site visit. This isn't a requirement for many similar certification/accreditation processes and yet I would suggest it is impossible to evaluate the culture of an organisation without speaking to business owners or senior executives 'eyeball to eyeball', speaking with employees and wandering unhindered – subject to any health and safety precautions, of course – around the premises. As I'll discuss later in this chapter, perhaps such a process may have alerted B Lab to potential culture issues at BrewDog before the company achieved B Corp status.

Social Enterprise

Perhaps you may have heard of the term social enterprise, often abbreviated to socent, and wondered what that means, or maybe thought you ought to be registered as one?

Social Enterprise UK, the membership body for social enterprise, defines social enterprises as:

> Businesses that are changing the world for the better. Like traditional businesses, they aim to make a profit, but it's what they do with their profits that sets them apart – reinvesting or donating them to create positive social change.

The Social Enterprise Mark, an organisation that launched an accreditation process to ensure social enterprises are delivering on their stated purpose, offers a similar definition:

> Social enterprises are businesses that put the interests of people and planet ahead of shareholder gain. These businesses are driven by a social/environmental mission and reinvest profits into creating positive social change.

There is no legal definition of a social enterprise, but it essentially means a business operates profitably, thereby enabling it to meet its social and environmental mission.

There may be additional restrictions according to how an organisation is constituted. For example, a Community Interest Company (CIC) requires an asset lock to be in place so that a social enterprise cannot sell its assets for private gain.

But I believe it is becoming increasingly evident that there may not really be any difference between a business that is registered as a social enterprise, either by the way it is incorporated or registered with Social Enterprise UK, and the sort of values-based, responsible business this book is talking about...

At the time of writing, I am the CEO of three CICs: Community Interest Companies registered with Companies House as social enterprises.

I love the ethos of social enterprise, but I have a love-hate relationship with social enterprise. Let me explain:

Social Enterprise: Politically Sexy but Not Picture Perfect!

Social enterprise is often described as the solution to the social and environmental challenges facing our society. It certainly might be part of the solution, and I applaud the numerous fantastic social enterprises across the UK that are driven by a social or environmental purpose. I love the whole ethos of social entrepreneurship. And as we all know, social enterprise is politically sexy, and there is cross-party support for the movement. But what about the elephant in the room...?

One of the big problems with social enterprise in its current format is the propensity for 'greenwashing'. Social enterprises often have access to considerable levels of funding or support that 'normal' businesses just don't have, and they are also favoured in public sector commissioning. But it is ridiculously easy to register a company as a social enterprise, and there lies the problem. How a business is constituted or labelled does not necessarily reflect that it is a responsible business.

Sadly, many of us have witnessed social enterprises (and charities) that are pretty good at delivering their core services but are astonishingly bad at looking after their people and considering environmental impacts. And yet numerous 'normal' businesses adopt responsible business practices on a holistic basis right across their company's operations.

There are nearly 5 million small businesses (small businesses being defined as those with 0–49 employees) in the UK that operate at the heart of their local communities. These organisations form 99 per cent of private businesses in the UK. This small business sector could provide an abundance of social value if gently incentivised to do so. And let us not forget that many of these small businesses already do a great deal to support their local community, look after their staff and reduce their environmental impacts. So why is there such an emphasis on social enterprise and not responsible business?

Social Enterprise UK (SE UK) says:

> The term 'social enterprise' came about from recognition that in the UK and across the world, there were organisations using the power of business to bring about social and environmental change without a single term to unite them.

Additionally, the organisation admits that:

> There has been a lot of discussion (and sometimes confusion) about what social enterprise is and whether the social enterprise label could be 'hijacked' by businesses that aren't social enterprises but are keen to pretend they are.

SE UK acknowledges the potential problem with the definition of social enterprise and generally takes a very pragmatic approach. For example, many funding bodies and other social enterprise bodies insist that a social enterprise has an asset lock. If public assets are being transferred to social enterprise and a considerable amount of grant funding is provided, then such an asset lock is a totally reasonable expectation. However, many social enterprises have been built on the back of the directors' sweat equity, which rightly should be reclaimable so that an asset lock would be totally inappropriate. SE UK fully acknowledges this.

Yet another issue is that many social enterprises continually refer to themselves as 'not-for-profit', which gives them a very unfair and misleading advantage. Social enterprises are businesses with a social mission. If they don't make a profit, they will fail. Even the CIC regulator states:

> The phrase 'not-for-profit' is frequently used when discussing social enterprises. This can be misleading and should only be used in the context of the company not having as its primary purpose the generation of profits for its owners. If a CIC fails to make profits from its activities (or in some way generate sufficient income to cover its running costs), it will eventually fail altogether. Therefore, rather than thinking in terms of CICs being non-profit making, they should be thought of as making profits for their community purposes.

And 'profit' is rather a moot point. We mostly think of profit in the context of PLCs making huge profits to pay big dividends and excessive bonuses to directors. But profit in its simplest form is left over from income after expenses, including directors' salaries, have been paid. For the majority of small business owners, their salaries are rarely excessive. Indeed, many small business owners earn less than the minimum wage if their work hours are considered! And it is standard business practice for any additional profit not drawn as salary to be ploughed back into the business to ensure its sustainability. No business can survive if this doesn't happen.

Naturally, directors of social enterprises should also receive a decent salary, and yet there is an assumption that owners of 'normal' small businesses earn far more than their socent counterparts. The reverse can sometimes be the case when a social enterprise has obtained grant funding that includes payment of salaries to help deliver a specific project.

So, let's look at some of the 'badges' companies use to be identified as a social enterprise, remembering the problem isn't the concept of social enterprise per se, but the unfair advantages socent has.

Members of SE UK using the 'We are a social enterprise' badge self-certify via a very short statement. I don't have a problem with this in principle as it is a similar concept to our basic ORB membership, albeit we do have a more in-depth questionnaire, our members are required to make a pledge, and the applicant will also be interviewed via a Zoom call. The problem is the perception of what the badge means.

A CIC is a special legal entity for social enterprises, limited by shares or guarantee, with a social mission statement and an asset lock. Although a specific legal entity, it is nonetheless very easy to attain CIC status.

To obtain the Social Enterprise Mark, an organisation has to evidence:

- It has social or environmental aims
- It has its own constitution and governance
- Earns at least 50 per cent income from trading (new starts have an extended time to reach this requirement)
- Spends at least 50 per cent of profits fulfilling social or environmental aims
- Distributes residual assets to social or environmental aims if dissolved
- Demonstrates social value

None of these examples requires evidence to demonstrate that the organisations in question are robust, efficient, ethical, compliant and responsible businesses!

The following case study is a good example of a social enterprise that I would not consider a responsible business that is actively making a positive contribution to society.

CASE STUDY

A few years ago, when I spoke with the director of a social enterprise that had applied for membership of ORB, he explained that the company was registered as a CIC and had recently received funding for a community café.

It all sounded extremely encouraging until I dug a little deeper.

The Community Interest Company Report (a short form that is registered at Companies House along with the Annual Accounts, which takes about 5 minutes to produce) described the company's key activities and impact as an organisation that was making homewares and essential household goods affordable for the local community in a very deprived area.

In reality, the business was founded on the 'pound shop' principle of selling cheap products with absolutely no social or environmental providence whatsoever.

And the community café? Obviously, opening a café was a pretty good ploy to draw locals into the shop for a cuppa and maybe a bite to eat and, naturally, have a look around the shop while they were there.

I suspect the owner has built a nice little business, especially with the bonus of grant funding. But it is just that. A business. Not a social enterprise.

Needless to say, I did not accept the membership application.

* * *

Isn't it time to consider how businesses actually operate rather than artificially giving precedence to a label that's politically sexy but not necessarily as picture-perfect as it is painted?

Isn't it time social enterprise and the 'normal' MSME business sector started working together to create real social change rather than treating each other with suspicion?

Isn't it time that delivering social value by considering people and the environment was accepted as Just Good Business rather than an exclusive club to which not all businesses can belong?

May I, therefore, boldly postulate that it is time for Social Enterprise (with a capital S and a capital E) to gracefully move back into the shadows and allow responsible business to be the defining element of the change in business operations our society needs. Of course, the responsible business movement will welcome social enterprises, charities and any other type of organisation to join the movement providing they are indeed operating as responsible businesses *across the whole of their operations.*

Social Value

Social Value as a term has probably been used on an ad hoc basis for years, but it was only when what is commonly known as the Social Value Act was introduced in 2012 that the term gained real traction.

The Social Value Act specifically relates to procurement in the public sector, discussed in a later paragraph, yet the term 'social value' has become a rather more generalised buzzword and, to an extent, a replacement term for CSR.

Social Value, in simple terms, from a business perspective, is the value that an organisation provides to society. However, Social Value UK offers a different perspective:

Social value is the quantification of the relative importance that people place on the changes they experience in their lives. Some but not all of this value is captured in market prices. It is important to consider and measure this social value from the perspective of those affected by an organisation's work.

Sounding complex? Indeed. But let's dig a bit deeper.

To a degree, one might argue that just by employing people, a company is delivering social value to that community. There may be a degree of truth in that, but if pay and working conditions are poor and no environmental considerations are in place, a business owner is actually lining his own pockets *at a cost to society!*

Social value should be viewed as the proactive approach to providing value to the community instead of what happens as a direct result of building and running a profitable business. It should therefore be a given that employees are well treated, so merely providing employment alone is not enough.

However, suppose an organisation adopts an approach that offers employment specifically to, say, ex-offenders or people with disabilities. In that case, that is clearly providing social value – although it should be a given that those employees are well treated.

A similar approach should be taken with apprentices, and some of the government projects launched periodically, such as the Kickstart Scheme. It is not always possible to employ people after such schemes come to an end but, especially with larger companies, the percentage they retain is a good indicator of whether there is a genuine intent to support people back into work or if they are merely maximising on cheap labour without providing genuine opportunities for career development within the company, or even the specific sector.

Conversely, companies that support young people or others furthest from the workplace by getting involved in mentoring schemes or offering work experience placements are clearly providing a great deal of value for potentially no direct return, albeit there is likely to be an indirect return.

A simple way to support the local community and provide social value is to help local people into employment and buy locally whenever possible. But there are multitudinous ways businesses can support their local communities, which we'll discuss later.

But why focus on measuring the impact?

For organisations such as charities and some social enterprises, there is a huge focus on measuring social value. For those organisations delivering direct services, that is totally understandable and, in most instances, not too difficult to achieve. If a charity has received a grant of, say, £10k, the funders will understandably want to know the societal changes resulting from the actions that £10k funded. So, not just what they did with the money but accurate accounting for the changes that happened and the importance of those changes from the perspective of those experiencing them. In other words, the funders want to know the Social Return on Investment (SROI)

In many large businesses, the CSR department or community committee are also likely to be required to provide a SROI report for the directors.

We take a very different approach aligned with the concept of ASTI – appropriate to the size, type and impact of the business – because, with micro and small businesses, the support given to the local community is invariably indirect. And even for a fundraising exercise where they would know how much they had raised, they would be unlikely to know precisely how that amount of money would be used and what societal impact it would create. Yes, they might be able to find out from the charity, but it's still a layer of additional work they do not need.

In 2014, under the umbrella of BSTLC (Businesses Supporting Their Local Community), a locally based sister company of ORB, we launched the Southend Business and Community Charter Award, which was backed by the local council, the local voluntary association, Southend Business Partnership and several other local organisations who, with two representatives from BSTLC, formed a charter committee and assessed the applications.

This is how the award worked:

1. Applicants had to work through the Responsible Business Workbook (now the online Responsible Business/Social Value course), self-assess and certify that they had reached the minimum requirements at the bronze level of 40 per cent. This was to ensure that they were operating responsibly across the whole of their business.
2. They then had to answer the following questions, providing supporting evidence:
   Q1. Awareness and commitment (understanding local issues and approach to offering support);
   Q2. Business Owners/Directors Involvement;
   Q3. Employee Engagement – not applicable for sole traders;
   Q4. Philanthropy (relating to financial philanthropy). This could be marked as not applicable because our focus was involvement rather than monetary support;
   Q5. Using local suppliers;
   Q6. Local staff – not applicable for sole traders;
   Q7. Supporting youth or disadvantaged groups into employment, such as mentoring, work experience, and apprenticeships.

3. We would complete an initial assessment in-house, score the application and complete a report.

4. Applications would then be finally assessed at a charter committee meeting, and our initial assessment would either be ratified or, in some instances, the scores and award levels amended according to the consensus of the committee.

The important factor throughout was that the committee looked at the application and assessed it, with an ASTI focus, according to what had actually been done over 12 months rather than trying to measure the social value of those actions.

CASE STUDY

Let's take the application submitted in 2018 by Emily Hewitt of I Am Emily Design and Marketing as an example.

At the time, Emily did not have any employees, although she worked with several freelancers on an ongoing basis and, as she always engaged them in community work, she chose to treat them as employees for the purpose of the application. This is a precis of her application, which was backed up with extensive documentary evidence:

Q1.Awareness

We feel it is important to contribute to our local area as our friends, family, and colleagues use these services at various points in their lives, and we want to keep that old-fashioned sense of 'community' alive, which is so often lost in today's society. It also benefits our business as we are seen as an ethical and caring company which, in turn, attracts the kind of people we want to work with. We are not after making big bucks on the latest trends in business; we would rather work with like-minded individuals who share the same ethics and values – we've found this promotes good relationships with clients that last and all whilst giving back to both local and global charities (only part of the response).

Q2. Business owner's involvement
A complete re-brand for Southend In Sight (previously Southend Blind Welfare Association), providing a new name, logo, brand, window and fascia graphics, website, business stationery and social media assets, all pro bono.

Pro bono marketing material for BSTLC.

Pro-bono website and rework of logo for SAFE (Supporting Asperger Families in Essex).

Pro-bono maintenance for Bosom Pals Southend website.

Supporting the Essex Wildlife Trust #30dayswildcampaign.

Mentoring sessions via the council scheme.

Q3. Employee Engagement
Freelances helped pro bono with the above, plus free print services to charities and videos for SAFE and BSTLC.

Q4. Philanthropy
Part of the B1G1 global cause marketing scheme plus corporate members of Essex Wildlife Trust.

Q5. Local sourcing
95 per cent of goods and services are sourced locally.

Q6. Local employees
95 per cent of freelancers used are local.

Q7. Supporting youth
Involved with Southend Council mentoring scheme.
FSB projects in schools such as birth of a business,
growth of a business.

* * *

Internally, we scored 29/33 and felt that was conservative! A well-deserved Gold Award was subsequently ratified without query by the charter committee.

I am sure everyone reading this would agree with that level of award for what was clearly a fantastic commitment to the local community, over and above what would usually be expected of such a tiny business.

However, if the award was based on measuring social value, how difficult do you think it might have been to get the required information? How long do you think that would have taken Emily? Do you think she would have even bothered to apply for the award if measurement was the requirement? Unquestionably not!

The Charter Awards are no longer operated locally but have been moved online as one of the national Responsible Business Standard certification options. The Social Value (Community)

Certificate follows much the same process, but all forms, together with supporting evidence, are submitted online and audited by one of ORB's external, trained auditors.

We want to encourage small businesses to do the right things, to provide social value to their local community, and we want to encourage them to apply for certification because that becomes a driver for other businesses too.

But we must retain a pragmatic approach. We must remember that in the context of micro and small businesses, the doing is more important than the measuring!

Social Value in Procurement

An important element of any legislation relating to public sector contracts is the ripple effect. Invariably, the main contractor will drive the principles of such legislation down their supply chains.

Evidencing you are socially and environmentally responsible when bidding for public sector contracts became increasingly important with the introduction of the Public Services (Social Value) Act 2012 and the 2014 EU public sector procurement directives. However, the legislation only required that social value be 'considered' and therefore, procurement departments in central and local government varied enormously in how they translated the social value requirement and the weighting afforded.

But the importance of social value in public procurement took a huge leap forward in January 2021 when Social Value in Procurement Policy Note 06/20 was implemented.

The policy note states:

Social value should be explicitly evaluated in all central government procurement, where the requirements are related and proportionate to the subject matter of the contract, rather than just 'considered' as currently required under the Public Services (Social Value) Act 2012.

Later that same year, due to the UK's commitment to achieving 'Net Zero' carbon emissions by 2050, the Procurement Policy Note 06/21 was introduced with effect from 30 September 2021. This requires bidders to demonstrate they have taken steps to understand their environmental impact and carbon footprint relevant to the contract delivery. As such, bidders must submit a Carbon Reduction Plan, which confirms a commitment to achieving net zero by 2050, including emissions reported for all required Scopes and environmental measures in place when performing the contract.

An important element of this is that Scope 3 emissions relate to indirect emissions, with a specific emphasis on the supply chain. Private companies increasingly require this information from smaller companies in their supply chain.

The weighting for social value in central government contracts must also be a minimum of 10, although it can be more.

Although these policy notes only apply specifically to central government, local authorities are gradually embracing the opportunity to add increased social value to contracts. However, some authorities are still struggling with the best way to implement social value and what value will be allocated to social value when scoring contracts. Additionally, procurement departments tend to be risk averse; thus, their approach to 'best value procurement' does not always reflect the views of local councillors and senior council officers. Nonetheless, this is rapidly changing, and social value will, quite rightly, play an increasingly important role in public sector contracts.

Thus, the emphasis on social value will continue to increase as public, and private sector organisations drive responsible business behaviour down the supply chain.

As small businesses are invariably best placed to provide genuine social value to their local communities, the growing importance of social value in public sector contracts is clearly an opportunity to be capitalised upon as the main contractor will also want to evidence social value in their supply chain.

But let's have a reality check here because I believe two aspects are currently missing in how social value is approached in procurement.

Firstly, the social value legislation mentioned above relates only to procurements covered by the Public Contracts Regulations 2015. In basic terms, these are larger contracts that have a value of £5 million per annum or above and are therefore more likely to be appropriate for bigger businesses, albeit quite often, small businesses may be specifically included in the supply chain.

Surely all public sector contracts, however small, should give social value due consideration? I believe this will happen in due course, but it can ONLY happen when it is easier to identify businesses providing social value. Currently, many public sector bodies actively, but sometimes mistakenly, give preference to social enterprises in contracts because they think that will automatically tick the social value box. That is why I believe small businesses not only need to be doing the right things but also be able to evidence that they are. I do not believe that because an organisation is incorporated as a social enterprise, it should have preference over any other type of organisation that is clearly demonstrating it is providing social value.

Secondly, there is nothing specific that looks at the history of a bidder to ensure the company has a history of genuinely delivering social value within the local communities where it is based or delivers contracts: the element of community social value scored relates specifically to what the contract is delivering.

In the Policy Notes mentioned, the environmental requirements necessitate a broader view of the bidder's approach to environmental responsibility and commitments, and while it will relate to how the contract is delivered, the requirements ensure that environmental considerations are embedded in the culture of the business.

But in terms of the 'community' aspect of social value, that is not the case, resulting in the potential for exploitation by businesses that do not have an embedded culture of supporting their local communities. For example, perhaps the bidder commits to employing x number of apprentices and x number of hours mentoring in schools as part of the contract deliverables.

So, perhaps the company may employ the agreed number of apprentices, but do they have a history of employing a reasonable percentage of those young people on a permanent basis once they have completed their apprenticeship period? If not, it suggests the company merely considers apprentices as cheap labour and therefore does not offer a high calibre experience with opportunities for career progression.

And does the company have a history of providing quality mentoring services or other comparable community support? If not, one might reasonably consider that they may not deliver to the extent that they have promised because, to be frank, checking that a company has delivered on its social value commitments is generally low down the list of priorities in terms of checking overall deliverables of a contract.

It would not be feasible for procurement departments to assess each company's historic social value contributions because of the diversity of each company and the diversity of the contributions they may have made. Increasingly, therefore, the importance of third-party social value validation will increase. I am very proud that ORB can already offer micro and small businesses robust Social Value (Community) Certification as part of the portfolio of Responsible Business/Social Value certification options.

In summary, although how social value is currently assessed in procurement is erratic, it is unquestionably an important aspect of the contract process that is likely to gain traction very quickly as a more enlightened approach to procurement is embedded across public and private sectors.

Socially Responsible Investing (SRI)

If you don't have lots of money to invest, you might think investing doesn't apply to you. But it probably does. Personal and workplace pensions are prime examples. Even a current account that is generally in credit is relevant in terms of how your bank uses those funds.

Historically, the basis for making investment decisions largely related to the best return on investment, regardless of where the funds were placed. Risk is fundamental to any investment decision as the value of stocks and shares can go down as well as up. As a first step, an investor would need to consider the length of time the investment is likely to be in place, as this can potentially level out any of the more volatile options, and whether they favour a higher risk option with potentially a higher rate of return, or a lower risk option with a lower return rate.

But for many investors, a new consciousness adds another dimension to investment decisions: socially responsible investing, sometimes called 'green' or ethical investing, is an investment strategy to invest money so that it provides an excellent financial return on investment, and also delivers social impact.

If you are engaging a financial advisor, do ensure they offer SRI options as opposed to the principle of 'do no harm' which relates more specifically to avoiding companies that make alcohol, tobacco products and arms, and more recently, oil and gas companies.

And do remember that pension schemes are some of the most prominent and influential investors in the UK, not forgetting that this also relates to workplace pensions. Wouldn't you want to ensure the pension fund in place for your employees is making a positive difference in society? Wouldn't your employees be pleased to know you have opted for a provider that will focus on SRI? (Although individual employees can generally individually request that their pension is moved to a different fund.)

Environmental, Social and Governance (ESG)

Another term you may come across is ESG.

ESG is a term developed in the world of investment to describe the nature of non-financial risk, which has operational and financial connotations. The three most significant risks are carbon emissions, pollution, and resource depletion, although many other potential risk areas exist, such as the company's internal controls, diversity and inclusion, human rights and labour standards, bribery, executive compensation and whistle blower programmes, as just a few examples.

Rather than the earlier approach of 'CSR projects', ESG will seek to establish a range of quantifiable targets across the whole of the business to improve its sustainability and lower its risk level across various factors. Unfortunately, the term ESG has started to creep into use in companies eager to say 'what we do is not just old-fashioned CSR' – although it often is.

The purpose of ESG should be to adopt a more rounded approach to 'good business', an approach we have embedded at ORB since we first launched, although what governance means in context of a small business is generally somewhat different to governance at a corporate level.

ESG criteria are of increasing interest to companies, their investors, and other stakeholders as a more reliable measure of risk and the ethical impact and sustainability of a company, particularly large organisations.

The environmental and social components are very clear and are elements we cover throughout this book. Governance is slightly different as the general approach adopted by sustainability practitioners relates to large organisations and includes factors such as executive pay; corruption; political affiliations and donations; board composition, diversity and structure; tax strategy.

Governance can be defined as the system by which an organisation is controlled and operates, including the structure and decision-making processes. At ORB, particularly within the requirements of Responsible Business Standard certification, we look at governance – although that is not necessarily what we call it – but with a pragmatic approach more appropriate for smaller businesses. Operating efficiently, meeting and exceeding legislation, having appropriate systems in place, and clear lines of communication are embedded in our holistic approach to responsible business.

ESG reporting is now commonly included in Annual Accounts. As yet, it is not a legal requirement, although mandatory climate-related financial disclosures by publicly quoted companies, large private companies and LLPs have been introduced for financial years starting on or after 6 April 2022.

It is very likely that both the scope of reporting requirements and the number of organisations affected by such legislation will increase unless it is evident that more companies are self-regulating and authentically paying due consideration to their social and environmental impacts. This will inevitably affect even the smallest of organisations as such requirements are pushed down the supply chain and expected by consumers.

B CORP

The B Corp movement, launched in the US in 2006 as a certification to evidence companies were a force for good, was started by three individuals. Two of the three were also co-founders of a basketball and clothing company with a reputation for being socially responsible. The company grew but stalled in 2005, at which point they decided to sell it. Almost immediately, all the values they held dear were stripped away, a common occurrence when a company is bought out that I will cover in the next chapter. At this point, the two men felt there was a need for a more permanent structure that would evidence and support the need for good social and environmental practices. Working with a former classmate who had been focusing on social change, they launched B Lab in the US, which retains the core responsibility for managing B Corp Certification and associated programs and software platforms across the globe.

B Corps stands for Certified B Corporations and is currently a highly sort after certification for businesses to show they are a force for good. The model is now administered in over 70 countries by individual B Labs, which are all separate entities affiliated to and using the same US-based central platform.

B Corp was brought to the UK in 2015 and is managed by the registered charity B Labs UK. B Corp has achieved almost cult status in the UK in the last couple of years, and the UK is the fastest growing country in the world for certification. However, there is an increasing concern among many about weaknesses in the system.

I mentioned the BrewDog debacle in Chapter 2. More recently, Nespresso, an operating unit of the Nestlé Group, has been certified as a B Corp, which has horrified many existing B Corp certified companies and other B Corp supporters.

According to Ethical Consumer, ethical issues with Nestlé include political activities, anti-social finance, possible use of tax avoidance strategies, animal testing, animal rights abuses, a poor approach to climate change and more. The company has also been the subject of the world's longest-running boycott by Baby Milk Action because, the group maintains, of the way that Nestlé 'aggressively markets baby foods in breach of international marketing standards, undermining breastfeeding and risking child health'.

It is not impossible for a company to achieve B Corp certification even if its parent company clearly would not, but Nespresso is not a brand most people would associate with being a force for good. As a colleague angrily declared:

> This monstrous Nestlé brand added a mountain of waste that did not previously exist and created an entirely new 'coffee vertical', which the world and his dog then piled in on with replica, wannabe pod coffee brands. All entirely anti-ethical to what the B Corp movement claims to stand for / be about.

Responsible Business Standard

ORB launched the Responsible Business Standard (RBS) in 2011, and it was therefore established in the UK before B Corp.

RBS certification works differently from B Corp, although the ultimate aim is the same: to drive the agenda for business to be a force for good.

Both certifications can happily co-exist, particularly as the RBS focuses on micro and small businesses. But for clarification, at this point, I would like to highlight key differences with the B Corp process:

1. In fairness, I will admit that B Corp's platform is far more technically sophisticated than ours. Nonetheless, the RBS is fully functional; it just doesn't have all the bells and whistles.
2. RBS is designed by a UK organisation for UK companies, includes UK legislation, and is presented in clear UK language. B Corp is very Americanised throughout.
3. RBS is designed specifically for small businesses, including freelancers and solopreneurs.

4. The B Corp process begins with the online B Impact Assessment with a company choosing the answer to a question from a list of options. The clever system shows you how many points each 'tick' would give you. The magic score to reach is 80, and you do not even have to answer all the questions. (Once submitted, the assessment is followed up with a robust process of telephone interviews and submission of appropriate evidence to support the responses, a process that is currently taking up to 2 years to complete.)

5. RBS begins with an online course before any of the certification options can be applied for. This can be seen as a barrier, but our ultimate purpose is to make a difference, and that is the aim of the course – to encourage people to think in depth about the questions in relation to their business and consider if they are doing all they should be and what steps they could take to improve. There is not a one-size fits all benchmark, although businesses can and should benchmark their own company using the ASTI approach I mentioned at the beginning of this book.

6. In the certification application stage, we do not offer multi-choice responses but ask open questions that require an individual, evidenced response.

7. To complete the highest level of evidence-based certification, businesses with five or more employees are also required to have an onsite visit, as that is the only way you can truly gauge an organisation's culture.

UN SDGs

The 17 UN Sustainable Development Goals are established as:

A blueprint to achieve a better and more sustainable future for all. They address the global challenges we face, including poverty, inequality, climate change, environmental degradation, peace and justice.

Clearly, this is a blueprint that every individual and every organisation should aspire to work towards because no one person or organisation can achieve those goals alone. Whatever role we play, whatever actions we take, however small those roles and actions may be, we are all part of a vast jigsaw, and if we all collaborate on making the world a better place, the picture of a better world will gradually evolve…

But as in countless aspects of life and business, individuals will look at these goals and instinctively think none relate to their life or their business; that the goals are far too big and complex for them to embrace.

This book does not explicitly work towards the UN Sustainable Development Goals, and yet, ultimately, the purpose is unquestionably to encourage businesses to operate in such a way that they ARE working towards those goals or, at least, specific goals that are most relevant to their business. Those aspirations and the actions thus taken will unquestionably be part of the jigsaw.

My default position is always a grassroots approach; I believe sustainable development is a journey, not a destination. I encourage all organisations, whatever type and size, to embrace every small step they take as part of that journey and understand that, rather like the ripples of a pebble in a pond, each of those small steps can have a far-reaching effect. And so, while I do not overtly refer to the UN Goals for Sustainable Development in this book, the journey you take is undoubtedly working towards them.

I, therefore, invite you to look at the 17 goals. Consider what they mean to you on an emotional level, and then consider how your actions or your business actions may be relevant.

1. No Poverty
2. Zero Hunger
3. Good Health and Wellbeing
4. Quality Education
5. Gender Equality
6. Clean Water and Sanitation
7. Affordable and Clean Energy
8. Decent Work and Economic Growth
9. Industry, Innovation and Infrastructure
10. Reduced Inequality
11. Sustainable Cities and Communities
12. Responsible Consumption and Production
13. Climate Action
14. Life Below Water
15. Life On Land
16. Peace, Justice and Strong Institutions
17. Partnerships for the Goals.

Remember that for each goal, no individual or single organisation can achieve the desired outcomes on their own: the concept is about the cumulative actions of many – the ripple in the pond – that will achieve the desired results.

Do think outside the box and consider what role you might be able to play for each action.

As an example, Goal 1 is No Poverty. Seven hundred million people live in extreme poverty worldwide, mostly in developing or war-torn countries, with a high concentration of extreme poverty in sub-Saharan Africa. We have all seen the heart-breaking images of poverty, hunger, disease and early death in these countries.

But surely, as individuals or small business owners, we cannot impact that situation.

Not true! Remember, every little action makes a difference...

Ensuring an ethical supply chain is one of the things you can do to safeguard against purchasing goods produced by slave labour. Fair Trade products, for example, ensure decent working conditions and a living wage for all workers.

But shockingly, there is also a great deal of poverty in the UK. Did you know that 4 million workers in the UK are living in poverty and almost half of them are in full-time employment?

Poverty is certainly not restricted to developing countries. In areas across the UK, even remarkably close to the most affluent areas, there are pockets of extreme deprivation.

Are there ways you could support staff if they might be living in such circumstances? Do you know if any of your employees need to resort to foodbanks, for example? Or could you support an appropriate local charity; or become a trustee for such a charity; could you offer to mentor young people at risk of exclusion to help them escape the poverty trap; or provide a young person with a first step on the ladder with work experience or even an apprenticeship?

What is significant about the SDGs is the need to take a holistic approach to sustainability. For example, Climate Action, defined as taking urgent action to combat climate change and its impacts, is one of the 17 goals. This reintegrates the environmental definition of sustainability into sustainability as a whole, giving it deserved weight as a fundamental and time-sensitive goal, yet no more vital than No Poverty, Zero Hunger and the 14 other goals.

No action taken is ever in isolation. Every action we take creates a reaction that may be either direct, indirect, or often both. And unless we are fully conscious of sustainability in its broadest sense, we are always at risk of creating adverse reactions that we are unaware of. Negative reactions could affect those closest to us or people in a different part of the world we may never meet or know. It is possibly in our nature to protect those immediate to us, yet increased globalisation, facilitated by the internet, means that the 'far-away' human consequences of our actions can stare us in the face in photos, videos, articles, etc., unlike never before.

Embracing a holistic definition of sustainability, which also resonates with what we call responsible business, recognises that prosperity should take the people and planet into account.

Prosperity will only endure if sustainability encompasses global needs across social, economic and environmental systems. Due to how vast and diverse the world is, we should look to our local context initially.

In other words, to quote a well-known phrase, we should 'think globally, act locally.'

Most individuals want to sustain a quality of life that is good for us, our families, and our local communities for now and future generations.

It is becoming increasingly apparent that the most honourable way to ensure that is possible is to embed personal, social and business responsibility into our choices, creations, and actions. It is not possible for a suffering population to enable environmental flourishing, just as humans cannot flourish on a suffering planet.

This impending problem should not immobilise us because a mindset shift has so much potential. Turbulent times can often drive disruptive, innovative change and unlock new sources of value and meaning.

And it is small businesses that are leading these changes because they are more nimble than larger businesses and can more easily adapt to change.

It is small businesses that are leading these changes – because business is personal!

Chapter 5 Who Controls Your Business?

I do, of course, I can hear you say indignantly! But it is not always that straightforward.

To clarify, we are not referring to control in the sense of micromanaging your team and every aspect of your business. That is an unhealthy approach that will disempower your people, suffocate creativity and create a more stressful working environment for you and your team.

This section is about ensuring your values are not compromised by external sources.

Rob Challis was Global Head of Corporate Responsibility at the Man Group PLC from 2003 to 2009. In 2009, he formed his consultancy, Tangent Synergy Ltd, which he continues to operate in conjunction with his work with several charities. Rob is another big fan of our work and was kind enough to deliver part of our training sessions for auditors for the Responsible Business Standard on a pro-bono basis.

Rob is quite a character and was particularly scathing of the tick-box approach to CSR that the big corporates adopted. He never minced his words, and one of his much-used expressions in his training was:

> Your stakeholders are anyone who can bugger up your business!

Take heed!

Assuming you have built your business on a clear framework of vision, values and a sense of purpose, as discussed in Chapter 1, how do you ensure internal or external influences do not sabotage those guiding principles?

How do you ensure that cultural DNA remains at the heart of your company as it grows?

Without a doubt, company values may change as your team grows and perhaps there may be a change of company focus, but those changes should happen as a result of the natural process of re-assessment as opposed to other factors causing loss of control.

A large part of exerting control and maintaining company values will relate to good internal and external communication. You certainly can't expect your people to live and breathe the culture you wish to instil if they have no idea what that is!

But let's look at other factors that can ambush your intentions.

Bootstrapping

Tony Robinson OBE, the author of *The Happipreneur* and founder of SFEDI (Small Firms Enterprise Development Initiative) and #MicroBizMatters Day, is a passionate champion of micro businesses. Although he spent many years in the corporate world, he walked away from the trappings of a luxurious lifestyle because he wanted to be true to himself. He wanted to choose whom he worked with, summed up by a very clear message to that effect in his book when he says:

Don't work with tossers!

Perhaps a few more subtle pieces of advice to start-ups are:

1. Bootstrap don't borrow – in the context of borrowing from banks and other institutions
2. Test trade first, preferably while still in a job
3. Ask for help from a business owner, particularly one that understands your customers

Bootstrapping means starting a company with personal savings and money borrowed or invested from friends and family.

Amazingly, many of the biggest companies in the world began as bootstrapped companies, with Apple, Coca-Cola, Dell and Microsoft among some of the most well-known.

But what happens if friends or family want a say in how you run your business, which is especially likely to occur if it appears to them – although they may be totally wrong – that your business is struggling?

What if you are not accepting certain contracts because the client is not aligned with your values, but your 'lender' wants you to accept the contract anyway because they are trying to protect their investment?

What if they want you to choose cheaper raw materials rather than the socially and environmentally conscious options of your choice?

A pithy but relevant biblical quote on this subject is:

> The rich rules over the poor, and the borrower is slave of the lender.

Having the 'Bank of Mum and Dad & Co' help you get started in business can be a huge financial benefit, but everyone must know exactly what the rules of the game are. I would suggest, at a minimum, you embrace these two suggestions:

1. Ensure your funders understand the values that your new business is being built on and that you will not compromise ethics and principles to make a quick buck! If your family and friends know you well, they should fully understand and respect your standpoint. If they do not understand, maybe you need to have many more values-based conversations with them about the importance of businesses having a positive impact on society.
2. Ensure you have a contract in place as protection and peace of mind for all parties involved: this is for everyone's benefit, not just yours. It doesn't need to be complicated, and you can draw something up yourselves, providing you ensure you get the agreement witnessed, but not ensuring clarity on all sides can be a recipe for disaster.

Bank Loans

Bank loans can be an appropriate way to fund your business, although they come with serious health warnings, not least that the interest rates and charges are often quite high, although still usually less than other online lenders, overdrafts, personal loans or credit cards.

One of the benefits of a bank loan is that you retain control of your business as opposed to equity finance, where you will be effectively selling a proportion of your business and, therefore, no longer have full control.

If you want a sizeable loan, most banks will require the loan to be secured against your assets, often your home. If you default, banks are rarely sympathetic and may start default proceedings surprisingly quickly.

The Royal Bank of Scotland has provided a rather unsavoury example of banks behaving badly with business loan customers. For six years following the 2008 financial crisis, many small businesses defined as 'financially distressed borrowers' were placed into the clutches of the bank's Global Restructuring Group (GRG). In 2018, the Treasury Committee published a scathing report that detailed systematic and endemic inappropriate treatment of small businesses resulting in financial distress, stating that GRG's overarching priority was generating income for RBS through made-up fees, high interest rates, and the acquisition of equity and property. These were businesses that were already struggling financially and thought the GRG would assist them by helping to restructure debts in a manageable way.

Even without the extremes of the RBS case, the inability to repay bank loans can result in actions being taken that might not fit with the company's core values.

CASE STUDY

I experienced that situation myself shortly after we launched ORB. We had negotiated a loan package via the local business development manager of, by chance, RBS. The agreement was that we would draw down an initial loan for pre-launch development work, and then, once launched, we would apply for two tranches of £10k that would enable us to employ two graduates in sales and marketing to help drive the business forward. This was all agreed upon in principle on the basis of the extensive business plan we had provided.

We launched in February 2010 and shortly after that requested the first £10k. Yep, said the BDM, I'll process that for you. NO said the system – your turnover is insufficient. We had just launched. Our business plan clearly showed that we needed additional funding to put people and systems in place to generate turnover. The BDM was genuinely distressed and tried to get the automated decision overruled but failed to do so.

And thus, we were left with a bank loan to repay but without the ability to drive the business forward in a way that echoed our business plan. Immediately, we were struggling to generate sufficient income for the company to be self-sustainable, including repaying the original bank loan, at that early stage.

We had many years of trials and tribulations, including an ever-increasing personal credit card debt. We were often in a position where we were unable to pay our suppliers in the 30 days that should have been the maximum. One of the saddest aspects of this situation was with one of our auditors, who we thought would be more understanding and supportive. Although we had explained the situation to him, he took umbrage that we couldn't pay his invoice on time, even though he was not financially challenged himself, and it destroyed what had previously been a very good working relationship. Naturally, he was paid in full when we could manage to do so, but the relationship never recovered.

It was a very tough time for us, yet it would seem we were extremely lucky not to have been one of those businesses referred to the GRG.

We worked through those tough times and are very proud that ORB is flourishing. Sometimes you just have to push through the pain and hold on to your dreams, but you can only do that if those dreams are based on a real sense of purpose.

* * *

Investors

Businesses with high start-up or development costs, and existing businesses wanting to expand rapidly, often look for equity investment rather than bank loans, as equity finance doesn't carry a repayment obligation. Providing the company is profitable, investors make money through dividends, i.e. a share of the profits, and by eventually selling their shares for, they hope, a significant profit.

The downside of equity investment is that the investor does literally own a share of the business. And anyone who regularly watches *Dragon's Den* will know that investors invariably want a big say in how the business operates. Even Deborah Meaden, the eco-queen of the Den, is only interested in investing in businesses that will provide a good ROI (return on investment) regardless of how 'green' the business is. (Although perhaps she is a more philanthropic investor when not in front of the camera – who knows?)

One of the recurring conversations with contestants is the question of the cost of raw materials/goods with Dragons making it abundantly clear that they could source the items at a much better rate. But what if the investor wants you to focus on price above quality, working conditions or environmental impacts? What if part of your raison d'etre for the company is to Buy British rather than cheaper produce from China, for example?

Investors are generally very experienced business people who know how to develop profitable companies. Many, although not all, are far more interested in investing in businesses they can help build and sell. Less are concerned about building a business where the priority is purpose above, or at least aligned with, profitability.

There is nothing wrong with building and selling a business, of course. And some people may even want to do that to specifically generate funds that support a more philanthropic purpose. But if the sole purpose of building your business is to build it and sell it for no other reason than to make a good profit, it is unlikely that your values will hold firm against the pressures of taking the most financially beneficial route.

There is a history across the developed world of successful, niche small businesses being purchased by big corporates that almost immediately change the way the business operates, moving the emphasis on people and the environment lower down the pecking order.

There are rare exceptions, one of the most notable of which is Innocent Drinks which is now almost wholly owned by Coca-Cola. I admit I'm not a fan of Coke, not because I don't like the taste – I don't particularly, but that isn't the reason – but because of the negative impacts the product has on the health of communities across the globe and their aggressive marketing practices, particularly in developing countries.

In 2007, War on Want said:

> Coca-Cola has been accused of dehydrating communities in its pursuit of water resources to feed its own plants, drying up farmers' wells and destroying local agriculture. The company has also violated workers' rights in countries such as Colombia, Turkey, Guatemala and Russia. Only through its multi-million dollar marketing campaigns can Coca-Cola sustain the clean image it craves.

> The company admits that without water, it would have no business at all. Coca-Cola's operations rely on access to vast supplies of water, as it takes almost three litres of water to make one litre of Coca-Cola. In order to satisfy this need, Coca-Cola is increasingly taking over control of aquifers in communities around the world. These vast subterranean chambers hold water resources collected over many hundreds of years. As such, they represent the heritage of entire communities.

Innocent Drinks is another example of a great company that started with the bootstrapping approach. In 1999, three friends spent £500 on fruit, turned it into smoothies and sold them at a music festival. While smoothies are everywhere now and many people make their own, it was a comparatively unknown product at that time.

Innocent Drinks was known not just for its great product but also for its socially and environmentally-aware ethos at the heart of its operations.

In 2009, many people, including thousands of loyal customers, took a sharp intake of breath when Coke bought a £30 million stake in the business, which, by then, had a turnover exceeding

£100 million and 275 employees. Everyone was convinced that the ethical practices embedded in Innocent's processes would be completely compromised.

But the founders were adamant that this provided an opportunity for the company to increase its positive impact, with co-founder Richard Reid pronouncing:

> Every promise that Innocent has made – about making only natural healthy products, pioneering the use of better, socially and environmentally aware ingredients, packaging and production techniques, donating money to charity and having a point of view on the world – will remain. We'll just get to do them even more.

In 2013, Coke increased its stake in Innocent Drinks to almost 100 per cent. The three co-founders stepped down from running the business but remained shareholders.

Yet it would seem that not only does Innocent manage to operate at 'arm's length' to its parent company with the promises Richard Reid made in 2009 still standing true, but Innocent has had a positive impact on Coke's approach to sustainability. Emilie Stephenson, who has been with Innocent since 2006, originally as a business development manager but now as UK Head of Force for Good, says the way the relationship is structured enables collaboration which can be mutually beneficial. An example is the development of 100 per cent plant-based bottles, with the prototype launched in 2021.

The moral of this example is that it is possible that equity investment, whether a small stake or a complete buyout, can be financially beneficial and still retain the core values of the smaller company, but it takes courage and strength to stand up to the potential investor and insist that contracts explicitly contain a detailed blueprint for how the company will operate under new ownership, including the values that must never be compromised.

CASE STUDY

As Jonny White, founder of Ticket Tailor, an event ticketing system, explains, he hadn't really considered investment for his new disruptive tech business. But when he did investigate the options, he decided investment was not a good fit for him or the company he was building. In this case study, he explains why he made that decision and is happy he did so.

But first, I'm going to take the liberty of a little shout-out for Ticket Tailor, the company we use at ORB for all the events we hold.

If you are a small business owner based in the UK and use Eventbrite to sell events, may I ask why? Agreed, it is a well-known, industry-standard event ticketing platform, but it is also a huge conglomerate with the ultimate controlling party, Eventbrite Inc. registered in the USA. Surely it would be more appropriate to use a responsible, UK-based company such as Ticket Tailor?

Perhaps Ticket Tailor's case study, in Jonny's own words, may even hasten that change.

When starting Ticket Tailor, I was very naive about the options around funding. My business knowledge didn't extend much beyond the children's book *The Elves and the Shoemaker*, where the more shoes he sold, the more that could be made.

Shortly after launching, with a couple of customers signed up, I went to a few local meetups to promote the company I was building. When I was asked, 'Are you bootstrapped, or are you trying to raise funds?' I didn't know what the term bootstrapped meant, and I didn't know it was an unusual decision to not try and raise funding to grow a tech business.

I explored the idea of raising funds as I began to understand it a bit more, as I must say the idea of having more cash in the bank when starting out was certainly appealing. However, investors aren't looking to put money into a business to take pressure off the founder, and it wouldn't have been a smart reason to take on investment.

We are now 11 years old and have grown slowly over the years to a team of 15 people and revenue of around £2m+.

The fact we are independent is a huge part of our identity today. It enables us to have complete freedom over everything we do. Firstly, our growth rate, whilst I'm very happy with it, could be considered slow for an investment opportunity. Secondly, what we choose to prioritise (sometimes over growth) is completely at our discretion.

Whilst we don't have investors, I am, of course, accountable: first and foremost to our customers, then our team, and lastly, the environment in which we are fortunate to operate in, whether that's Hackney the borough, London the city, UK the country or this glorious planet.

When I look at other heavily funded, stock-market-listed, market-leading tech companies in this industry, I'm not envious. Many report millions of dollars of revenue each year, without ever making a profit and instead consistently report millions of losses. It clearly isn't sustainable, and in my mind, a loss-making business is a failing business.

I'm incredibly excited that we have got Ticket Tailor to a point where we can afford to start giving back. For every ticket sold, we donate 1p to climate causes. In 2021 this meant a donation of £66,000, and we are aiming for £100,000 in 2022. Giving back in this way makes our work feel like it's worth so much more, and it's an example of where we are using our freedom to choose something else over growth.

It's worth noting that we didn't get to this position overnight, and it wasn't my original ambition for the business to necessarily be a force for good. Initially, I needed to pay the bills, then I wanted financial security (both for me and the business), and then wanting to put what we had to good use. The point is that what I wanted from the business on day one is very different to today, now that it is established, and I have greatly appreciated the freedom to change objectives.

Solopreneur Is Fine

Many entrepreneurs start a business with the intention of growing it. Or you may be launching the type of business that needs employees right from day one. That is fine, of course. I love to see start-ups succeed and expand.

But equally, I love that many freelancers and solopreneurs are happy to retain the business on that basis, i.e. with no intention of employing any staff.

Some people adopt a rather strange perspective that labels all solopreneurs, regardless of whether they are working full-time or have launched a part-time side hustle, as having a 'lifestyle business' that is somehow not really a proper business.

Firstly, if more people had better life-work balances, the world would be a much happier place.

Secondly, over seventy-six per cent of private businesses in the UK have no employees. And a large percentage of those businesses are highly successful and profitable. There is definitely nothing second-rate about being a solopreneur. Similarly, no one should feel embarrassed that they work from home – or a coffee bar, a park or even the beach! Richard Branson has always worked from a home office. When building Virgin, he lived on a houseboat with his family and, he says, would happily go seamlessly from taking an important call to changing a nappy.

But the most successful solopreneurs rarely work alone. They invariably outsource elements of their business operations to others with the appropriate expertise, such as bookkeepers, virtual assistants, web designers, and social media managers.

Additionally, solopreneurs often collaborate on contracts with others in a similar or complementary sector.

In all cases, but particularly when collaborations take place, it is essential that you ensure you are working with people who not only have the appropriate skillsets but whose values are aligned with your own; who are totally committed to the project you are working on together and will always act as a great ambassador for your business.

If you do not consider all these factors, the relationships you have built/are building with your clients and your business reputation could very quickly be sabotaged.

And it really is not fun working with people who do not share your values, so ensure you maintain control!

Small Is Beautiful

I have already outlined my passion for micro and small businesses and their potential for making the greatest positive societal impact. Perhaps this is a good point to consider the work of the esteemed E. F. Schumacher, author of the 1973 book *Small is Beautiful: A Study of Economics as if People Mattered*. In 1995, this was ranked by *The Times* as one of the hundred most influential books published since World War II.

Small is Beautiful is a collection of essays based on these prevailing principles:

We cannot consider the problem of technological production solved if it requires that we recklessly erode our finite natural capital and deprive future generations of its benefits

1. Individuals need good work for proper human development
2. Capitalism brought higher living standards at the cost of deteriorating culture
3. Large cities and large industries would deplete natural resources
4. The development of non-capital-intensive, non-energy-intensive society as opposed to ever-increasing growth
5. Universal prosperity alone cannot ensure lasting peace
6. Education is one of the greatest resources providing it instils the right values
7. Nuclear energy could be mankind's most dangerous invention

The following are a few quotes from *Small is Beautiful*:

Modern man does not experience himself as a part of nature but as an outside force destined to dominate and conquer it. He even talks of a battle with nature, forgetting that if he won the battle, he would find himself on the losing side.

Of helping men and women to achieve independence from bosses, so that they may become their own employers, or members of a self-governing, co-operative group working for subsistence and a local market...this differently orientated technological progress (would result in) a progressive decentralisation of population, of political and economic power.

An attitude to life which seeks fulfilment in the single-minded pursuit of wealth – in short, materialism – does not fit into this world because it contains within itself no limiting principle, while the environment in which it is placed is strictly limited.

Yet all really important innovations and changes normally start from tiny minorities of people who do use their creative freedom.

Any intelligent fool can make things bigger, more complex, and more violent. It takes a touch of genius — and a lot of courage — to move in the opposite direction...because from bigness comes impersonality, insensitivity and a lust to concentrate abstract power.

Schumacher was born to a family of academics. During his early adulthood, he studied economics and was a committed atheist. However, an open and enquiring mind fed by a broad range of literature and research, coupled with worldwide travel where he would immerse himself in the culture of the local people, led to a change of heart and adoption of Christianity.

Schumacher described Gandhi as the greatest 'people's economist' whose economic thinking was compatible with spirituality as opposed to materialism.

Schumacher suggested that all communities and regions should be as independent as possible; otherwise they are politically and economically vulnerable, an approach I find shockingly prophetic because Russia's unwarranted and devasting invasion of Ukraine is financed to a large extent by the oil and gas it sells to the West. On 4 May 2022, the EU proposed further sanctions on Russia, including banning Russian oil imports, although not gas, by the end of the year. It is expected that because some EU countries are so dependent on Russian oil, they will likely veto the proposal. Food prices are rising across the West as fuel prices continue to soar. Additionally, as Russia and Ukraine provide over a quarter of the world's supply of wheat and 80 per cent of sunflower oil, there is a knock-on effect on the price of bread, dairy, meat and many other food basics.

Schumacher was an early proponent of renewable energy, and his was one of the first homes in the UK to have solar panels installed. He was also deeply concerned about soil depletion and agricultural systems based on monocultures and oil-based chemical fertilisers.

Schumacher died suddenly in 1977 at the age of 66. Sadly, the approach he termed Buddhist Economics was largely dismissed by his contemporaries during his lifetime and is still at odds with current economic and political policies. However, his work continues to influence people and organisations worldwide directly and indirectly. For example:

The Schumacher Society was founded in 1978 to:

advance the education of the public in the teachings of Dr E F Schumacher as they relate to issues affecting the future of our local and global society, including resource use, climate change, environmental management and social cohesion by organising and facilitating cross-disciplinary learning and the funding of research, the useful results of which will be disseminated for the public benefit.

In 1980, the Schumacher Center for a New Economics was founded to:

envision the elements of a just and regenerative global economy; undertakes to apply these elements in its home region of the Berkshires in western Massachusetts; and then develops the educational programs to share the results more broadly, thus encouraging replication.

In 1986, the New Economics Foundation (NEF), which is based in London, was founded with the aim of working for a:

> new model of wealth creation, based on equality, diversity and economic stability.

NEF has given birth to a range of initiatives including, but not limited to, the Ethical Trading Initiative, AccountAbility, Time Banking UK and the Community Development Finance Association.

It would be inaccurate to claim that this book, and my work at ORB, are based on the work and philosophy of Schumacher. Nonetheless, our approach mirrors the principles he so ferociously espoused, particularly our belief that small businesses have the greatest potential to make this world a better place.

Tony Robinson OBE is also a huge fan of Schumacher, succinctly summing up his work thus:

> Ernst F. Schumacher published *Small is Beautiful: Economics as if People Mattered* in 1973 – nearly fifty years ago. He conjectured then that many large corporations would never say 'enough' and would exploit employees and suppliers, engender inequality, and destroy our communities and the planet.

In 2017, Tony and Tina Boden founded the 'Small is Beautiful' Roll of Honour, a list of businesses which signed up to the following values:

1. #PayIn30Days ALL suppliers ALL the time

2. Promoting equality and diversity
3. A fair day's work for a fair day's pay
4. Protecting our environment and communities
5. Unlimited growth is pathological
6. Small can make a difference and should be supported

Tony recognised that a small number of large corporations and many medium-sized businesses, along with most small and micro business owners, do believe in Schumacher's 'Small is Beautiful' values and that it is essential that we recognise these organisations and choose to do business with them.

I was delighted when in 2022 because our values echo those they are so passionate about, Tony and Tina gifted the Small is Beautiful Role of Honour to ORB to be embraced within our membership.

Tony is a huge supporter of ORB and continues to be one of our valued Advisory Board members and, more recently, a director.

As Your Business Grows

But if you do want to grow your business, how do you ensure you maintain the values that are important to you as you build your dream team?

Yet again, much relates to communication. If you are communicating your values internally and externally, and in job descriptions, you should find that people interested in the role are more likely to be aligned with your purpose.

A simple mantra to always bear in mind in the recruitment process is:

Hire for attitude. Train for skills.

Some positions need people with specific expertise, experience and qualifications, which should never be overlooked. But in most instances, skills can be taught. Sometimes, according to the position, it can be preferable to proactively try and employ people without existing sector-specific experience so that they can be moulded more effectively to a role rather than bringing bad habits learnt at a previous company with them. Alternatively, they may be looking for a new role because they did not like or approve of how an existing or previous employer worked, and your espoused company values appeal to them.

Also, remember the value of transferrable skills. Many graduates, in particular, have degrees in subjects totally unrelated to the positions they eventually pursue and adapt extremely quickly and effectively to new roles.

Attitudes can be changed, but that will only happen if individuals acknowledge their negative or disruptive behavioural traits and want to change. And that change can only happen if supervisors and managers help empower employees to make positive change rather than trying to enforce change, which is more likely to lead to confrontation, increased stress and potential disruption for everyone.

Also, consider the benefits of employing a diverse range of people with different backgrounds and viewpoints that not only have a good culture fit but whose unique personalities and experiences can enhance and enrich your company culture.

Clearly, it is best to ensure people have the right attitude from the beginning: individuals whose personal values align with the company's culture. When that happens, the right team will take ownership of shared successes, and your people and the company will thrive. Get it wrong, and you could find morale, motivation, and team cohesion all plummet.

To ensure the right culture fit when going through the employment process, you must ask appropriate questions at the initial interview. A good way to start might be to say to the interviewee:

Tell me about yourself and what is important in your life.

If you feel unsure about undertaking this sort of interview, try Googling 'values fit interviews' or 'culture fit interviews', and you will find loads of helpful articles and videos to enable you to plan an effective interview structure.

As your business grows, delegation is essential. This is often an area entrepreneurs struggle with. Many end up micromanaging because of their innate viewpoint that no one can do a job as well as they can. Ensuring you build the right team with the right culture fit and appropriate skills, whether existing or trained, should help alleviate those concerns.

Supervisors and Managers

If your business continues to grow, you will likely introduce new supervisor or manager roles. While the instinct is generally to promote someone reliable and good at what they do, that is by no means the only consideration. Introducing this new layer of responsibility without acknowledging the broader picture and the implications of having the wrong person in a more senior role for which they have neither the appropriate skills nor behavioural traits can be a recipe for disaster, with company culture slipping surprisingly quickly.

Jim Clifton and Jim Harter are senior executives at Gallup, a global analytics and advice firm that 'helps leaders and organisations solve their most pressing problems' and are joint publishers of the Wall Street Journal bestseller *It's the Manager*. The book is based on Gallup's largest study on the future of work.

The full title of the book is:

> *It's the Manager: Gallup finds the quality of managers and team leaders is the single biggest factor in your organisation's long-term success.*

This staggering statement is backed up by their extensive research, which shows that a staggering 70 per cent of the variation between great workplace engagement and lousy workplace engagement can be explained just by the quality of the manager or team leader.

Why does this happen?

So often, an individual will be promoted because they are good at their job, and are then just shown how to complete the administrative element of their new role.

But because someone is good at what they do does not automatically make them a good leader. So often, these individuals feel compromised because they feel their priority is increasing productivity. And although that may be true to a degree, the best way to increase productivity is not through micromanagement and lack of empathy.

If a business is values-based and the culture is embedded throughout the organisation, it will be a more equitable and happier workplace. And the most productive employees are happy employees who find meaning in the work they do and the company they work for.

New managers need to be trained on how to maximise human potential, a process that should be totally aligned with the company culture. As *It's The Manager* explains, good managers should be coaches, not bosses. They need to focus on the strengths of employees and help them develop and utilise those strengths in their career progression.

In terms of weaknesses, they too need to be understood and acknowledged. But rather than finger-pointing, constructive criticism and providing appropriate self-development support are more likely to produce positive outcomes.

It is a rare individual who can move up to a supervisory/ managerial level and immediately understand and exhibit the emotional intelligence required by their new role. It is therefore absolutely essential that appropriate training is provided otherwise the culture you hold dear can be damaged very quickly and the results potentially catastrophic.

CASE STUDY

Adnams PLC has a history going back to 1345, with beer being brewed on the site in Southwold, Suffolk. Adnams as a company was established in 1890, and family members remain on the board to this day. From those early beginnings, the company has grown from a small brewery to being distillers, wine merchants, retailers, publicans, hoteliers and, of course, brewers, with over 500 employees.

From the beginning, the company was built on a set of embedded values that they have retained throughout their journey. In this case study, CEO Andy Wood OBE DL explains the positive impact maintaining those embedded values has had on business growth, development and the extraordinary challenges faced by the hospitality industry during the COVID-19 pandemic. He says:

> In the context of this book, Adnams is not a small business. That said, it has more in common with smaller businesses than global giants in that it sees itself rooted in its community, and it is always from this base that it builds its business.
>
> Adnams Plc is something of a hybrid in that the majority of its shares are held amongst families, staff and pensioners but it also has a listed element to the business with the majority of those shares being owned by small long-term investors. It is this financial structure that enables Adnams to adapt its purpose led, values driven approach and means that it can invest in its people and its assets for the long term.
>
> The tangible business benefit of this approach was particularly evident during the COVID pandemic. As most people are aware, the hospitality industry was one of the hardest hit during a period of lockdowns of varying degrees in 2020 and 2021, but being purpose led and values driven meant our team were totally committed throughout and that we were able to support our pubs with rent cancellations for 18 months. Ironically, we've

probably emerged stronger, more together and fitter but never complacent.

Adnams is serious about communicating its values to staff, customers, investors and wider stakeholders. With one of its values being Sustainable Success the construction of a new distribution centre in 2006 was a means to communicate the commitment in a real and tangible way. The building was designed to maximise environmental performance and so every opportunity was taken to reduce the impacts of the building. Unique at the time, a local supply chain was activated to ensure the materials used travelled the shortest possible miles necessary to arrive on site. The building itself was built seven metres down in a disused gravel workings which limited the visual intrusion on the landscape and provided thermal stability. The building was then constructed from a wooden frame and lime hemp blocks because of their thermal properties. The roof is supported by 90m end-to-end Glulam beams and then topped off by a Sedum roof. The building benefits from solar panels and rainwater harvesting system. Many of these technologies were new to industrial buildings in 2006 and in the 15 years since completion the building has maintained an ambient temperature in its main warehouse of around 14 degrees C, the optimal temperature for the storage of cask beer. Whilst the upfront cost may have been 20% more expensive than a standard metal warehouse seen close to major motorways, the savings in energy usage have more than compensated with its roof actually sequestering co2 from the atmosphere. The building is a prime example that good business need not cost the earth.

When it comes to people, Adnams has an enviable track record of developing its own. Karen Hester joined the company in 1988 in a part-time role as an office cleaner. Her commitment to the company soon shone through, and Karen moved into clerical roles, latterly leading a team of delivery drivers and warehousemen as Transport Manager. Karen excelled in this then male-dominated environment and was the CBI's East of England Business Woman of the Year in 2013 and joined the board of Adnams shortly after in the role of Chief Operating Officer. The company is committed to developing staff and believes talent is abundant within its workforce and that it will shine through if the right conditions are set and the right encouragement given. Karen's story proves this and is a further example of the company bringing its values to life.

Customers and Suppliers

Whom you sell to and buy from can greatly impact your ability to retain the values you want to maintain in your business.

The fashion industry is a prime example. If your customer wants cheap, fashionable goods that they are happy to discard after just one season and a limited number of wears, you will struggle to maintain any significant values.

Currently, because of the laws of supply and demand, products that are the most sustainable in terms of both production and lifespan are likely to be more expensive. Gradually, this is likely to change. In the interim, if you want to uphold your values, it is important to attract customers who are prepared to pay a little more for goods and services that can demonstrate social and environmental providence.

For some, deciding to sell into a marketplace with a slightly higher disposable income might seem contrary to their values of supporting the most disadvantaged. A little bit of creative thinking is required here. This will vary according to your product or service, but building a successful, profitable, values-based business will open doors for you to give back in so many different ways, as the following case study demonstrates.

CASE STUDY

Seffie Wells launched aidie London in 2018. The company was developed because of her inability to find the quality of baby shoes she wanted for her son. She says:

> When my son was a baby learning to walk, I realised there were no shoes that supported his early development. I could only find hard, structured shoes. With a background in Psychology, I incorporated my knowledge and set about designing a pair of shoes that would mimic barefoot walking and therefore enhance his opportunity for optimal development. That's when aidie London was born.

I was delighted when aidie London became members of ORB just a few months after launching the company and have been proud to watch the company go from strength to strength, gaining a horde of accolades along the way, including, but certainly not limited to, being named 'Most Trusted Baby Clothing & Products Company of the Year 2019' at the SME Business Elite Awards.

From those first walking shoes, aidie London now stocks a range of baby shoes plus sleepsuits, muslins, blankets, bibs, socks, booties, books, and so much more. They are beautiful, sustainable products – but they are certainly not the cheapest baby products on the market.

From the beginning, Seffie was determined to launch a brand that not only provided products that were good for babies in the here and now, but also helped to protect their future by embracing environmental sustainability.

But that is only part of the narrative. Seffie had her own background story that was driving her to not only succeed with her new business but enable her to really make a difference in an area she was passionate about.

As a young mum, Seffie fled her home, with her baby, to a women's refuge to escape domestic abuse. She saw first-hand the challenges mothers with new babies faced when living in these circumstances.

In 2020, Seffie launched The Aidie Trust to raise awareness of domestic abuse and help to protect vulnerable babies across the UK.

The trust provides support and guidance to pregnant women and young mothers who have fled domestic abuse, donating baby essentials, care packs and grants to new and expectant mothers in women's shelters.

The Aidie Trust is supported by UNICEF UK's Baby Friendly Initiative to provide the most up-to-date research and advice in infant care following periods of trauma. A percentage of profits from every sale of aidie London's products is donated to the trust.

What Seffie has achieved in only a few short years is incredible and speaks volumes for her foresight, commitment and resolve in developing an outstanding baby brand that enabled her to support a cause that was very close to her heart.

* * *

Ensuring your suppliers are aligned with your values is essential. Having the right suppliers can help enforce your values but get it wrong, and all the good work you do could be compromised.

I have already mentioned how social and environmental considerations are being driven down the supply chain and how this will impact how small businesses need to show they are meeting specific standards. But small businesses also have their own supply chains, albeit not generally as extensive.

As a small business, how do you ensure your suppliers meet the environmental standards that are part of your messaging?

How do you ensure that your suppliers also meet good social practices, particularly if you are in the fashion, food and beverages, or consumer electronic sectors?

In 2020, several high-profile companies were hauled in front of a Parliamentary Committee to address claims that their suppliers might be using forced labour in direct contravention of the UK Modern Slavery Act 2015.

Supply chain scrutiny can be challenging but checking your suppliers' credentials, asking appropriate questions and making it abundantly clear what your expectations are, is essential.

But a word of warning when checking credentials: do make sure they have value. I was recently told by the owner of a small company that he could only remain in one of his biggest client's supply chain if he attained a specific accreditation. On the face of it, that sounds like an excellent way of driving social value down the supply chain. Unfortunately, the 'accreditation' in question merely consisted of a two-minute, online, tick-box exercise – and I am honestly not exaggerating – whereby if you answered yes to ten questions, you were accredited!

ORB's database is littered with applications for membership from companies that have completed and 'passed' our online questionnaire, which is the first step to applying for membership, and yet those membership applications have not been accepted. Why? In many cases, it is blatantly obvious that the applicant has just ticked the highest scoring response to all the questions, and further research has shown they have been less than honest! We do not accept membership based on just the questionnaire. And that is just membership. We make it abundantly clear that membership alone is NOT a certification or accreditation.

The particular organisation offering the credentials I have mentioned is trying to encourage ethical business behaviour but is unfortunately misguided. What they are actually doing is opening the door to greenwashing. As we all know, and as we have certainly experienced at ORB, many not-so-ethical companies would tick yes to those boxes if they felt it would benefit their company.

I am not naming the organisation offering these unwarranted accreditations, as I hope they will change the wording from accreditation to pledge. And a pledge is good – but clearly not the same as evidencing that you are genuinely meeting the requirements of a robust certification process.

But there are also some organisations whose intentions are not so virtuous. They are more intent on cashing in on the requirement for credentials that evidence social or environmental standards and offer awards/certifications/accreditations that are not based on credible evidence.

And as an aside, you may wonder what the difference is between accreditation and certification.

To be brief, certification verifies that an individual or organisation has achieved a certain level of competence in a specific area against set standards; accreditation means that an organisation has received third-party recognition and approval *to be able to offer a certification process.*

However, in practice, the two words are used synonymously. I have long given up trying to stress or worry about the differences and the way the words are used, providing there is real credibility behind the processes involved to gain such certification or accreditation.

Business Consultants and Advisors

I don't have a problem with business consultants and advisors per se. I know many who are superb. Indeed, many are members of ORB and everything they do within their own businesses and when working with clients resonates with the responsible business mantra. But the type of 'business expert' who hasn't adapted to today's changing business world drives me nuts. And sadly, I think far too many business consultants fall into that category. You know the type I mean? Guys, and it is primarily men, who are still preaching tired old mantras that were seen as appropriate maybe ten years ago but no longer fit the demands of a more open and transparent society. The 'business experts' that still focus on Friedman's approach to business rather than caring about people, planet AND profit.

Good business consultants can provide invaluable support and advice for start-ups and growing businesses because most of us are not experienced in all aspects of running a business. And however much we know, there is always more to learn and a different approach to consider. But do take care when choosing a business consultant. Ensure they understand and support your values, will be a good fit for the business you want to develop, and are very clearly committed to providing advice specifically aligned to meet and enrich your stated values.

I passionately believe that business consultants should not be allowed to provide advice funded by a public body unless they have committed to a triple bottom line approach which is why ORB includes an option in our CPD and Monitored Self-Assessment Certifications for business consultants to make an additional pledge to do just that.

The following case study is an example of a business consultant I would advise values-based businesses NOT to engage:

CASE STUDY

Several years ago, I spoke with a young man at a business networking event. Paul really impressed me. He had started his business several years previously, primarily as a gardening service. Having grown his company over several years, he was, by then, providing a wide range of contract services from grounds maintenance to commercial cleaning services.

We started talking about the products Paul was using, and I was pleased he chose eco-friendly options whenever possible. He was excitedly talking about how his business was growing and that he didn't lock organisations into long contracts when a business consultant joined the conversation – as happens in the ebb and flow of business networking. We'll call our consultant Alistair for the purpose of this exercise.

Paul continued to explain that his customers liked the fact they weren't locked into long-term contracts, and it had been a real differentiator for him. He said he believed he could keep clients by providing good service and value for money and, therefore, really didn't see the need to insist on longer-term contracts, although he was moving from one month's notice to three months because of the staffing situation.

Alistair frowned and stated in a rather smug tone:

> Yes, I can see that's a good way to build your business, but it isn't good for the longer term. You need to start thinking about locking your clients in for a much longer

period. If you want to sell the business or get additional funding, you will need to show that you have those long-term contracts in place.

I replied:

I totally disagree. All Paul needs to be able to do is evidence his current contracts and be able to very clearly demonstrate that he maintains his clients even without long-term contracts. That is a far better indicator of the company's integrity and worth than being dependent upon locking in clients for the longer term.

Well, the look on Alistair's face said it all! Clearly, he was a long-established business consultant who knew how these things should be done. What on earth was I talking about?

I think our conversation may well have degenerated into a bit of a spat, but for another delegate unwittingly extracting me at that point from the discussion.

Paul had developed his business on the principle of trust. And it was working extremely effectively for him. Without question, it would continue to work, providing he maintained a quality service.

Honesty, courtesy, trust and fairness create a mutually harmonious relationship. Paul had adopted a comparatively rare approach, but not unique, as we shall see in a later chapter. But had he engaged that consultant, the very essence of his business could have been compromised.

Chapter 6 Marketing

What Makes a Brand?

Your brand is so much more than your logo, company colours, the style of literature and websites. These considerations are, of course, extremely important, but as a company develops, its branding is more about reputation than an attractive logo. People's perception of a company becomes all-important, remembering that 'people' includes everyone the business comes into contact with, including employees, customers, suppliers and the wider community.

Let's be very clear, the value of most businesses is not the assets on the balance sheet – the value of a business is in its reputation.

That has been all too apparent with big companies where a damaged reputation has had huge financial implications, sometimes even bringing about its downfall. Remember the demise of Ratner's the jewellers when the CEO Gerald Ratner described his products as total crap? Or Arthur Andersen LLP, once one of the 'Big Five' accounting firms, whose reputation never recovered from criminal charges brought against the company relating to Enron – even though the guilty verdict was subsequently overturned.

Jeff Bezos, the founder of Amazon, allegedly said:

> Your brand is what people say about you when you are not in the room.

And Linda Ganksy:

> A brand is a voice, and a product is a souvenir.

These statements apply to businesses of all sizes, from a sole proprietor to a multi-national, more so than ever with our 24/7 media-driven society.

So, what is the reputation of your company? What do people say about you and your business when you are not in the room? How do you ensure you maintain and continually enhance your reputation?

Perhaps most importantly, consider again if your business is built on clear principles and an ethical culture. Are values an important part of the business DNA? Protecting your reputation is an essential element of risk management in a business, and enhancing your reputation deserves a clear strategy.

And Don't Hide Your Light Under a Bushel

When we launched the Southend Business and Community Charter in 2014, we were amazed at the number of businesses that do support the local community in a variety of different ways, but so often completely under the radar.

Is it the natural English reserve that stops business owners and directors from shouting about their good work? Apparently, some people even feel it's morally wrong to promote their business on the back of their 'good deeds'. Others are frightened of being accused of greenwashing, and others just haven't thought about it or got around to doing anything about it.

But I would absolutely encourage businesses to shout out about the good things they are doing, authentically, of course. I would love to see them blowing their own trumpets. Why? It's pretty simple, really:

* * *

DOING GOOD IS GOOD FOR BUSINESS

Firstly, we genuinely believe that if a business is supporting the community, it should gain the business benefits from doing so. Businesses that are authentic in their good works do what they do because they feel it's the right thing to do, and it gives them pleasure. And that's absolutely the way it should be. But that shouldn't mean they can't or shouldn't promote their good deeds. Customers would love it, and it certainly helps increase profile and reputation. And in some cases, as I have already mentioned, it is even a requirement of businesses that are tendering for contracts.

But the second reason is perhaps the most important. Please, please don't hide your light under a bushel because the more businesses talk about the good stuff they do to support their communities – whether that's fundraising, volunteering, mentoring or employing apprentices – the more it will become mainstream. There are so many terms bandied around: social business, CSR, shared values...The ultimate goal is not for businesses to have a special label: the ultimate goal is that 'doing good' is the norm: that it's viewed as *just good business.*

Green Claims Code

The Green Claims Code became effective on 1 January 2022, but it is not new legislation as such.

Since the launch of commercial TV in 1955, advertisements have been controlled by legislation. From 1988, the ASA (Advertising Standards Association) was able to refer advertisers who made persistent misleading claims to the OFT (Office of Fair Trading) for legal action.

From 1995, the ASA's remit was extended to cover 'non-broadcast electronic media' and further extended in 2010 to cover an advertiser's marketing communications on their websites and other non-paid space such as social media.

In 2013, the CMA (Competition and Market's Authority) was formed to take over the functions of the previously existing OFT and Competition Commission and, among other things, is responsible for protecting consumers and enforcing consumer protection legislation.

The rapidly increasing awareness of environmental issues has resulted in a dramatic increase in demand for more sustainable goods and services, presenting a welcome commercial opportunity for a new breed of environmentally conscious companies to serve that marketplace. Unfortunately, it also makes it attractive for less scrupulous, or sometimes rather less well-informed, companies and marketers to try and claim a competitive advantage by inappropriately differentiating a brand or product as 'green, eco-friendly, sustainable', or any other similar term.

The surge of eco and green advertising and increase in consumer complaints, together with an international analysis of websites suggesting that 40 per cent of green claims made online could be misleading, has led both the ASA and CMA to focus very clearly on the 'green' arena and make it abundantly clear what is and is not acceptable.

The CMA published the Green Claims Code in September 2021 as a guidance document and a clear warning that as of 1 January 2022, it would be enforcing the law.

The approach is still to help and advise rather than take immediate enforcement. However, it has been made abundantly clear that companies intent on misleading consumers and who are persistent offenders will be treated very severely.

An early case illustrates how even companies such as Alpro (UK) Ltd that are genuinely trying to do the right thing sometimes get it wrong.

On a large poster on the side of a bus, Alpro pronounced that its plant-based milk alternatives were 'Good for the Planet'. This was challenged and the complaint upheld by the ASA because there was little context provided in the ad with which to interpret the claim and, they concluded, it was therefore ambiguous (in the context of other information on the poster), misleading and breached the code.

I have spoken very specifically about green claims, but this is also likely to embrace claims relating to social responsibility. So, while we do encourage marketing to showcase the good things you are doing, it is essential that you are not only authentic but also accurate and can substantiate any claims.

These are the six key elements you must consider in marketing, advertising and branding:

1. Claims must be truthful and accurate
2. Claims must be clear and unambiguous
3. Claims must not omit or hide important information
4. Comparisons must be fair and meaningful
5. In the claim, you must consider the full life cycle of the product or service
6. Claims must be substantiated

Who Are You Then?

I don't know about you, but I get really frustrated when I am on a website and cannot find any information about the site's owner, and often I cannot even tell in which country the company is based.

When that happens, I'll leave the site pretty quickly, even if it provides the goods, services or information I am looking for.

I am sure other people feel the same. Websites with just a mobile number for contact or, worse still, only an automated 'contact us' email box do little to inspire confidence. Any business that isn't transparent enough to say who they are will likely lose customers.

But they are also likely to be breaking the law as it is also a legal requirement in the UK that certain business information is displayed:

Company details to be displayed by incorporated organisations:

- On the business premises, a sign with the company's full registered name that can be easily seen.
- The full legal name should also be included on all hard copy and electronic documents, including websites.
- On order forms, business letters and websites, the following should be displayed in addition to the full legal name:

  ◦ The place of registration
  ◦ The registered number
  ◦ The address of the registered office
  ◦ The legal structure

Company details to be displayed by sole traders:

- The business trading name, which may be just your name, and the registered business address should be clearly displayed on business premises, most business documents, and websites.

Note that this is your registered business address which is not necessarily the same as your home address. Many sole traders naturally prefer not to disclose personal address details and use their accountant's address or a mailbox service as their registered business address.

People like to know whom they are dealing with, so make sure your contact information is readily available. Check your website today and add any missing information, so you are totally transparent. Don't lose any more customers – and don't break the law!

Regarding websites, don't forget that there are many other requirements, including cookie and privacy policies.

Cause Marketing

Cause marketing is a fantastic way of collecting money for charities and community groups as it raises the profile of both the good cause and your company.

Cause marketing is where you pledge a fixed amount or percentage of sales or turnover, either across the board or for specific products or projects, and this is prominent in your marketing.

But it is important to remember that if you are using the name of a charity in your marketing, it is a legal requirement that you have a Commercial Fundraising Agreement (CFA) in place.

If you are working with a local charity or community group, this is usually comparatively easy to set up and agree to. You do not need a solicitor, just a written and signed agreement of the terms of your commitment and how you are permitted to use the charity's name in your marketing.

But if you want to fundraise for a large, national charity, that is more difficult unless you are a big corporate committed to raising vast sums of money. For small businesses, it is better to use a platform such as Work for Good. It is free to join, takes just a few minutes to set up your agreed commitment online, and all the legal stuff is automatically taken care of.

Another popular platform that works in a similar way is B1G1, a global platform with a more significant focus on supporting developing countries rather than local charities.

Whichever option you choose, cause marketing is a fantastic way to show the world what you stand for, inspire your team and build deeper relationships. And when you know your work will help a cause close to your heart, it becomes personal and rewarding. You put more of yourself into it; you take more pride in it.

That's what inspired founder Rupert Pick to set up Work for Good in the first place. When Rupert's daughter Ottie was born ten weeks premature with two rare genetic conditions, he decided to donate all the fees from his next workshop to the Evelina London Children's Hospital that had looked after her. And that made him wonder about all the other amazing things that could happen if it was easier for more businesses, especially smaller businesses, to give through their work.

That's what makes the Work for Good or B1G1 approach so much more powerful than a simple cash donation: it puts giving at the heart of your business.

And it can help businesses engage with their clients on a deeper level. More and more, people want to deal with socially responsible businesses. By letting their clients choose which charities to support, businesses can make them feel like they're part of the story too.

However, as we always stress, businesses can support their local community in numerous ways: it doesn't have to be about giving cash, and I would encourage you to think creatively in this respect. Adopting a cause marketing approach is to be commended, but it should not be used on its own as an easy way to tick the community engagement box.

Niching

If you have ever attended a marketing workshop, you will no doubt have been told that you need to ask yourself the following questions before you develop your marketing strategy:

- What problems do you solve for your customers?
- Who is your perfect customer? (Demographic, specific habits, goals and priorities, communication preferences, career, industry, gender, pain points, etc.)
- Could you focus on niching by segmenting your markets?
- What is your specific area of expertise?

The essence is that if you have not clearly identified your perfect customer, you could potentially be wasting time and money marketing to individuals and companies that are never likely to be interested in your products and services.

I am extremely excited to witness the birth of a new breed of marketing: niching in a way that says loud and clear:

'I only want to work with companies that are aligned with my values.'

How this is packaged and the words used varies, but this type of niching is invariably the key feature displayed eloquently on their website.

Most importantly, the companies I am talking about here are not specifically in any of the ethical/social or environmental sectors because clearly, their potential clients are either already passionate about those issues or, at a minimum, eager to improve and embrace change.

No, these are 'ordinary' businesses: accountants, copywriters, business consultants, virtual assistants and many more.

It is a brave step, and I know many people who have taken this step have initially been very nervous about doing so. But the results have been amazing. These businesses have thrived not only financially but also physically and mentally in an environment where working with like-minded people provides pleasure on a daily basis.

Below are three examples of small businesses in different sectors that have taken this step. There are loads more I could share. It is a big step to take, but the more we define who we want to work with, the more we'll drive the movement for a better way of doing business, so please do consider how you might be able to be more selective in who you work with.

As you will see, two examples showcase vegans who proudly showcase what is important to them. Neither is saying they will ONLY work with vegans, but all these examples are very explicit in who they will work with.

CASE STUDIES

Chaos Into Calm, an online business management company, is not only flourishing but is expanding both in the number of employees and associates and also the range of services offered.

Founder Sam Roblett explains why she decided to focus solely on working with ethical businesses and the impact it has had:

My reason for starting Chaos Into Calm was to make an impact. After researching the damage animal products cause to animals themselves, the environment and our own health, I made the decision to align my actions to my ethics and go vegan.

The information I learnt showed me how much of what happens is hidden from view with clever marketing. We aren't told about how products reach our homes and our plates. I was convinced that if people knew these things too, they would choose kinder options, and so I began to talk to family, friends and co-workers.

This was harder than I thought, and people acted like I had been indoctrinated into a cult. At times I felt like I couldn't be who I really was or express my feelings about things fully. I couldn't believe people would think that choosing to live my life with the least harm possible could be so radical, but this is a symptom of how our world has evolved.

So, I hit the streets. I joined my local animal rights and environmental activism groups and used my strong communication skills to talk to strangers. But after four years, it still felt like things weren't moving fast enough. I wanted to make more of an impact, and I wanted to help people see that there were more ethical options to choose. As consumers, we make choices and exercise our power through the products and services we purchase.

This got me thinking…in order to make choices, those better choices needed to be available. With more ethical options readily available, the public would have no excuse but to choose the compassionate option. But with such a high number of businesses failing in the first five years, we needed to make sure that success happened for those businesses that held strong ethics towards animals and our environment.

I founded Vegan Business Networking on Facebook and LinkedIn to sow seeds of collaboration and support for each other, and started my online business management company, Chaos Into Calm, with our aim being to support ethical business owners to continue and grow at the point where everything becomes too busy and overwhelming for them to succeed alone. Chaos Into Calm provides strategy, business systems, operations management, sustainable development and team support. We have helped values-based businesses succeed when they otherwise would have given up due to lack of structure, organisation, resource and overwhelm.

The vegan, ethical and plant-based market is tough, everything a business does is under greater scrutiny, and they must set themselves the highest levels of integrity. For me, working in this niche and choosing who I will and will not work with means that I can truly live and work in harmony with my ethics. I get to work with inspiring people who want to do more than make profit, they want to change the world. They are here to make an impact, and we are here to help them succeed.

*   *   *

Write Rabbit is a copywriting and content company launched by Tash Morgan-Etty in 2019 when she emigrated to England. Here she explains how her personal 'Aha!' moment came when challenged by a client she was working with.

Protecting nature and helping people were ingrained in me as a child. However, although these passions followed through into my private life and hobbies as an adult, I hadn't found a way to link them consistently to my work life.

During my careers in TV production, journalism, corporate communications and marketing across Africa, I had pushed environmental and social agendas as much as I could but quickly became frustrated at how siloed CSR often is, as well as the common perception of it among management as nothing more than fluffy PR coverage.

In 2019 I took the opportunity of emigrating to England to switch my career to copywriting – something I'd wanted to do for some time. Having excitedly gone about setting up my company and putting the word out there, a sustainability expert approached me needing help with his content planning. He proposed a skills exchange whereby he would help me green my business in exchange for a content strategy. I was sceptical about the idea as I didn't think there was much about my business that could be 'greened'. I worked entirely from home on a laptop, after all. I'm pleased to say he proved me wrong! He showed me that there was plenty I could do to improve my business and positively impact the planet. At one point in the process, he challenged me to consider using my services to support planet-positive clients.

That was my 'Aha!' moment.

Within days I'd pivoted and niched down to focus on brand messaging and writing for companies with an eco-friendly and/or ethical ethos. So, rather than having a siloed CSR arm or doing random bits of work to support youth or environmental organisations, I now had a business driven entirely by a positive purpose.

I can't say it was an easy decision, but – having registered the company just a couple of months prior to the Covid-19 pandemic and having no real network within the UK anyway – I figured I didn't have much to lose. From a strategic point of view, talk of sustainability was rapidly on the rise, and the focus on healthcare worldwide highlighted the cracks in social systems. So, I knew that the demand for planet and people-friendly marketing messages was only ever going to increase. But, to be honest, I mainly made this change because it felt right.

How has it worked out? Well, like a lot of early-stage businesses, it was a bumpy start. However, as soon as I began networking in the same circles as other ethical businesses – through organisations like The Good Business Club, the Better Business Network, and the Organisation for Responsible Businesses – and focusing my marketing on the most relevant social media channel for my audience (LinkedIn), the enquiries began flying in.

Of course, leads aren't the only measure of success. Aside from steadily building a positive reputation among the types of businesses I serve, the most rewarding result of niching into this space has been the people. It's not something I'd thought about when I'd pivoted, but it's been great to find that fellow business leaders operating in this space are genuinely the loveliest bunch of folks you could ever wish to meet. The fact that I get to work directly with them and support their purpose-led missions feels like a huge privilege.

I'd strongly encourage anyone considering focusing on supporting this sector to give it a go. I look forward to welcoming you to the Light Side.

* * *

The Vegan Publisher, founded by Mitali Deypurkaystha, is a book consultancy and publishing company dedicated to helping vegan, ethical and responsible business owners put their mission, movement and message on the map so 'together we can change the world, one book at a time.' But as Mitali explains, that was not always the case:

When I started in 2020, I was a publisher for all kinds of business owners. I've been vegan since 2012 for ethical reasons, and I loved the idea of working with vegan, ethical or responsible business owners. But 'nailing my colours to the mast' frightened me. What if it put off some people from working with me? What if I was niching down too far and my business would fail because of a lack of customers?

The turning point came in May 2021. After releasing my book, *The Freedom Master Plan*, I was inundated with messages from many vegan, ethical and responsible business owners asking me to join their networks. They would question why I did not mention anywhere in my book, website and social media that I was an ethical vegan.

I realised that I'd been foolish. I'd made a very basic mistake in business. And that is, when you try to appeal to everyone, you end up appealing to no one. From that day on, I decided to focus on working with people who align with my values.

My clients don't have to be vegan to work with me. In fact, more than 50 per cent of my clients are not vegan. But they are ethically minded, value-driven and strive to do the right thing when possible. Publishing a book is a momentous occasion, and if your book is raising awareness and creating a bigger impact, it makes sense to work with someone who believes in your values as much as you do.

I've been able to double my business within a year. I also rebranded as The Vegan Publisher from Let's Tell Your Story Publishing (although that still is an imprint) and released the second edition of *The Freedom Master Plan*, specifically for vegan, ethical and responsible business owners.

Not only that, making the conscious choice to work specifically with value-driven business owners allowed me to come into contact with incredible people who have furthered my understanding of what more I can do. For example, I got to know a vegan and ethical design company who then designed my website so that it emits a tiny 0.29g of carbon per page. I'm currently talking with an ethical payment gateway that promises to plant a tree per transaction. The list goes on.

Every day, I'm inspired and uplifted because I've chosen to surround myself with people who have the same drive to create a fairer planet. I've made lifelong friends. When you have the same values, it's inevitable!

I wish I knew back in 2020 what I know now. When you stop trying to please everyone and focus on what is right for you in terms of your values, you start to attract what you deserve in abundance.

Chapter 7 The Workplace

Many of you reading this book will be sole proprietors with no employees. It might therefore be appropriate for you to skip this chapter – BUT wait...!

I would recommend you read this chapter for two key reasons:

1. Think of yourself as an employee and aim to consider the best ways to keep yourself fit, healthy and motivated.
2. A high percentage of small businesses work on a collaborative basis with other small business owners. Yes, it is a different relationship, but, nonetheless, replicating the core principles of best practice in the workplace will help ensure the most productive, reciprocal relationship.

Responsible business should start in the workplace. If your staff are not happy and engaged, you cannot expect to effectively implement other aspects of responsible business. And if you did try to do so, it would be inauthentic.

Your staff should be your greatest asset, yet we all know that managing people is not always easy. Employing staff can be challenging. There is a minefield of rules and regulations to abide by, and sometimes workplace dynamics are far from straightforward.

Thinking of your workplace as a league football club is often a clever way of developing an overarching strategy.

- The club endeavours to employ the best players: players with the right skill sets, but who are also team players

and will fit in with the ethos of the club and the existing
players.
- To ensure best performance, the right players must be
in the correct position, continually train to retain and
improve their skills and fitness levels, and their general
physical and mental wellbeing should be prioritised.
- Every player knows their role, how they should interact
with their teammates, and how to cover other people's
roles if needed.
- Everyone needs to know and understand the rules of the
game.
- Referees ensure the rules of the game are adhered to, and
a system is in place to address issues with unruly players.
- Managers should be able to engage, motivate and nurture
players, and also deal effectively yet empathetically with
underperforming players.

In summary, a good workplace has a solid foundation based on
the rules (legislation, HR policies and procedures), which helps
employees and their managers understand what is expected of
them. Implementing best practice ensures continual engagement
and motivation.

Understanding and managing people is a vital part of a
manager's role. Yet, in the workplace, individuals are often
promoted to a supervisory or management position without
being provided with appropriate people management training.

Legislation
While I agree that certain legislation is excessive for a small
business, and the government is indeed taking steps to lessen
that burden, compliance is nonetheless essential; otherwise, it
puts the company at risk.

Workplace legislation is continually changing, and keeping up to date with legal requirements can be extremely challenging.

As a small company, you may not be able to employ specialists in each area. It may therefore be worth considering outsourcing certain aspects such as HR and Health and Safety legislation. Alternatively, becoming a member of one of the larger business organisations such as the FSB (Federation of Small Businesses), FPB (Forum for Private Business), IOD (Institute of Directors) or an industry-specific trade association, all of which should provide excellent resources and ensure their members are kept up to date with changes in legislation.

But while I have stressed that rules must be in place to protect both the employer and the employee and to ensure fairness and consistency, a dedicated, motivated and productive workforce will owe more to 'best practice' than to rules and regulations.

Staff need to feel they are valued: their achievements should be recognised; they should be treated as individuals. Senior management should interact with staff and share information and ideas with them so that they can play a role in company development. Your line managers need to be effective in their roles and have had appropriate 'people' training. Being good at a job does not necessarily dictate that they are good at people management.

Your staff should be your greatest asset, and if you treat them well, not only they but also your business will thrive. These are just a few of the potential benefits:

- Better staff retention rates
- Increased productivity levels

- Better quality of work
- Improved customer service
- Lower levels of absenteeism
- Lower levels of presenteeism
- Better relationship with management
- More innovation

Do remember that a happy employee will be one of the company's best advocates as people naturally talk about the things they enjoy (as well as the things they don't!) Happy employees will spread the word about the good things your company does, improving its reputation and making it easier to recruit the best talent.

Employee Health and Wellbeing

Most business owners understand it is a legal requirement to consider the health and safety of employees but do not realise this extends to their broader wellbeing, and specifically mental health wellbeing.

In legislation, considering employee health and wellbeing is often described as having a 'duty of care'. But as health and safety expert Malcolm Tullett vehemently states in his book *Risk it: How to use your intuition to revolutionise risk taking*:

Care is not just a duty.

We should care about our employees because, well, they are our employees, and therefore we care about them. Just as we care about our friends and family and not because it is a duty to do so.

Nonetheless, it is important the legislation is adhered to.

All employers with five or more employees should have a written health and safety policy and risk assessments that are relevant not just to employees, but to any other people who could be affected by company activities.

Even if you have one employee or work with contractors, it is worth starting as you mean to go on and ensure such policies are in place, remembering that 'workplace' means anywhere a person usually works, which may also include their own home.

I believe it has been one of the positive outcomes of the pandemic that more employers have accepted that allowing their people to work from home can be mutually beneficial, despite the UK government's subsequent messaging post lockdowns that they want employees to stop working from home and return to the office.

For some employers, allowing their people to work from home permanently has become the norm, although a greater percentage have adopted a hybrid working model. But this does not work for everyone. Some people just do not have the proper facilities or struggle with isolation. Or perhaps they have other challenges and cope better in the social and supportive environment colleagues can provide.

Mike and I have worked together in our home office for nearly 20 years, and I love it. But, in fairness, our house is big enough to accommodate a proper working environment, we don't have children or any other dependants at home to worry about, and we are quite happy being together 24/7. Well, most of the time. We are not immune to the odd squabble!

In response to a more permanent move to working from home, the HSE (Health and Safety Executive) has introduced new legislation which emphasises that if the home environment is not suitable, or cannot be made suitable, and the employee cannot be reasonably protected, they should not be asked to work from home.

The key to protecting the health and wellbeing of employees is culture, communication and training.

If an honest, open and trustworthy culture is a genuine way of being that is embedded throughout the company rather than just a 'policy', many potential challenges will be automatically averted. But for this to be truly the case, as I have already mentioned, care needs to be taken to ensure that people are employed based on matching values, and team leaders are trained in the skill of empathy because, as training and leadership coach Bruna Martinuzzi says:

Empathy is the oil that keeps relationships running smoothly.

Nonetheless, more needs to be done to proactively support the wellbeing of your people both at a whole company level and individual focus.

Ongoing training for all staff is an imperative. Training can and should take the form of skills training and self-development training, both of which will help ensure staff are capable of accomplishing the requirements of their role and provide them with the potential to progress in their careers.

Training can take many forms from formal external workshops, onsite courses, and on-the-job training. It does not need to be expensive.

Naturally, induction training is essential and should include familiarisation with the job role, deeper discussions about the company's culture, and appropriate information about policies, including health and safety, all of which should ensure the employee knows exactly what is expected of them. If possible, ensure all relevant company policies are readily accessible online. Give your new employees plenty of time to read and absorb the documentation, ensure that they have done so, and encourage them to ask questions if there is anything they are unsure about.

In terms of legislation, all employees should have written contracts of employment and written disciplinary and grievance policies should be in place. And from the minute you take on your first employee, you must ensure you have Employer's Liability Insurance and set up a Workplace Pension Scheme.

Having more comprehensive HR policies in place can seem unduly onerous, but the clarity they afford can make life much less complicated as minor behavioural issues often create the biggest tensions. For example, company policies relating to mobile phone use, social media and even cigarette breaks might not initially appear to be the most essential policies to have in place, but why wait until there is a problem before you consider and document what your company policies are?

Good communication and clarity at an early stage can avoid many future 'misunderstandings', but there also needs to be a more formal structure around staff appraisals, for example. I'll hastily add that these appraisals should not be akin to many corporate practices where the primary purpose is measuring performance against KPIs (Key Performance Indicators.) Such appraisals often cause significant stress leading up to the event and how they are conducted.

Staff appraisals should be a mutually positive experience. They should be part of a healthy relationship between employees and managers rather than what might feel like a rather officious affair. And perhaps most importantly, a good line manager will realise if one of the team is not performing well this, in the majority of cases, is an indicator that the employee has a problem which may be internal or external. That should be the time for a discussion rather than waiting for an 'official' six-monthly or annual appraisal. But the discussion must be along the lines of empathy, support and finding solutions rather than finger-pointing and blame.

Every employer, however small the company, is legally required to have at minimum a suitably stocked first-aid kit, an appointed person to take charge of first-aid arrangements, and the details of such arrangements provided to all employees. According to the size of the company and the risk levels, you may be required to have a trained first-aider.

Similarly, consider the benefits of mental health first-aider training for yourself and all managers, even at a very early stage. It is not a legal requirement, although it is a recommendation. But stress is such a common health issue, and regardless of how that stress is caused, mental health first-aider training will make a tremendous difference in recognising the symptoms and offering appropriate support.

Both first-aider and mental health first-aider training will provide transferable skills that can be hugely beneficial outside the workplace.

Time, cost and physical restraints will limit what a micro business can offer its people in terms of health and wellbeing initiatives. Nonetheless, there is much that can be done for even the smallest business. And that includes looking after yourself if you are a solopreneur.

The same applies to benefits you may offer employees. As we have already seen, millennials are less likely to be impressed by a shiny salary package than by an organisation's culture. Consider, therefore, if possible, the type of benefits that extol company values, such as:

- Flexible or hybrid working
- Cycle-to-work schemes
- Volunteering options
- Holiday trading schemes
- Environmental or community focus groups
- Salary sacrifice schemes.

At the very minimum, you should aim to pay the UK Living Wage as set by the Living Wage Foundation. For employees aged 23+, this is slightly higher than the National Living Wage set by the government, but the rate also comes into force for employees over 18, whereas the NLW has reduced rates for 18-20- and 21-22-year-olds. Additionally, the UK Living Wage includes a London weighting.

However, I do recognise that even that is not possible in certain circumstances.

As an example, Joan (not her real name), the CEO of a flourishing enterprise agency, was achieving fantastic results in her local town by negotiating with landlords to take empty properties and set them up as hubs for small businesses, resulting in a growing number of start-ups and a vibrant high street. Some of these developments included community cafés, enabling the agency to offer employment, training and support to various groups of people. Joan spoke about a young man employed at one such café and said she could only pay him the minimum wage because the café would be running at a loss otherwise.

Hence, she compensated in as many other ways as she possibly could. As he was 19, that basic rate was then £3.07 per hour less than he would have received on the Living Wage basis.

Sometimes, we have no option but to cut our cloth according to the situation. Most people agree that genuine appreciation for a job well done, sometimes just manifesting in a simple 'thank you', is often worth more than a financial reward. And if finances are challenging, staff will invariably not expect more than that. Once again, communication is key.

However, there is a vast difference between paying someone at a lower rate and trying to compensate in other ways because circumstances dictate the necessity of doing so, than paying the lowest legal rate purely to reduce overheads and increase profits. That situation is particularly unpalatable when senior executives are taking excessive salary packages.

And as I touched on previously, taking advantage of funded schemes or lower-paid options such as apprenticeships is acceptable if you are genuinely training the employee and providing them with appropriate skill sets to support their future career development, and with the intention of employing them at the end of the scheme if possible, rather than blatantly using such employees as cheap labour.

According to The Equality Trust, CEOs in the UK's top 100 companies enjoy an average salary of £5.3m each year, an astounding 386 times that of an adult earning the National Living Wage.

Now I know many small business owners probably earn less than the National Living Wage if you fully consider all the hours worked, and most will probably never aspire to an annual salary in excess of even £200k. Nonetheless, considering what you pay yourself and ensuring it is not excessive in comparison to the salaries of your lowest paid workers is something any ethical business owner should take seriously.

Most do. Many pay their employees more than they earn themselves. And that is yet another reason why micro and small businesses should be celebrated and supported.

Equality and Diversity

As I'll discuss later in this section, a diverse workforce can be highly beneficial for a business. But it is also essential to be aware of legislation relating to discrimination.

While I would certainly hope that anyone reading this book would not intentionally discriminate against a specific sector of society either in the workplace, in any other business relationships or on a personal basis, it is important to be aware of legislation so that you do not inadvertently appear to be discriminatory when that was never your intention.

In the UK, although it is not a requirement to have an Equality and Diversity Policy, it is against the law to discriminate against anyone in the workplace because of a protected characteristic, including the following:

- Age
- Disability
- Gender reassignment
- Marriage and civil partnership
- Pregnancy and maternity
- Race, ethnic or national origin, colour and nationality

- Religion/belief/lack of any religious belief
- Sex
- Sexual orientation

It is also against the law to discriminate during the recruitment process, including in job adverts.

Neither should you ask about health or disability unless:

- There are necessary requirements of the job that cannot be met with **reasonable adjustments**
- You are finding out if someone needs help to take part in a selection test or interview
- You are using **'positive action'** to recruit a person with a protected characteristic

You should not ask for anyone's date of birth on an application form unless they need to be a minimum age to do the job (which would be considered a genuine occupational requirement).

Generally, applicants do not need to tell you about **criminal convictions that are spent** (there are certain exemptions, such as when applying for positions in schools).

Although it isn't a legal requirement to have an Equality and Diversity Policy, it is undoubtedly advisable. Additionally, if you are applying for public sector contracts or grants, such a policy is inevitably a requirement.

But what are the benefits of a diverse workforce apart from policies and legal requirements?

People often describe having a diverse workforce as having 'a melting pot of fresh ideas'.

Rather like the football team scenario at the beginning of this chapter, a business needs people with different talents and abilities. People from diverse sectors of society and with different backgrounds will have different thought patterns, ideas, problem-solving methods, and mental perspectives. Research continually evidences that teams with this broad cultural diversity are more likely to be effective at problem-solving and delivering a constant stream of out-of-the-box, fresh ideas.

A trap many of us fall into is unconscious bias. It is a natural human trait to gravitate towards people we have a lot in common with, who think and act like us. And while it is important to ensure employees have values that match the company's ethos, a monoculture of staff that think and act the same can result in a lack of innovation and low employee morale.

Once again, however diverse a workforce, maximum benefits will only be materialised if there is an excellent communication flow and people at all levels are engaged and motivated.

That all said, I am not generally a fan of positive discrimination. When we recently had a Kickstarter vacancy at ORB, I proactively made a position available for a young lady with physical disabilities as so few opportunities were open to her. But we have a very small team, and I would not have proactively tried to find a placement that was, say, a person of colour or from the LGBT community just to tick the 'token diversity box'.

And I do think some people are far too quick to make inappropriate judgements, such as a personal experience I had recently.

ORB has an Advisory Board which, by necessity, consists of professionals with considerable expertise in their specialisms.

A large part of the AB role relates to ensuring the Responsible Business course and certifications are kept up to date with legislation and best practice.

One day, a lady told me that she had considered applying for membership of ORB but wouldn't because the Advisory Board was overtly white and middle-class. I was so taken aback that I don't think I could give a coherent response.

Was I guilty of unconscious bias, I asked myself? I dug deep, and my conclusion was that I wasn't, and a very unfair assessment had been levied against me. Let me explain why.

We had eight people on the Advisory Board, ages ranging from the early thirties to early seventies. No youngsters, to be fair, but we need experienced professionals for this role, so a pretty good age range.

We had six men and two women. Not quite equal, but it's a small group.

Middle-class? Well, they are all professionals, so you could probably say that, although I certainly don't think they are all 'wealthy middle-class'.

Sexual and religious persuasions? I haven't got a clue. Why would I?

The only thing we did not have is anyone of colour. (We include board member pictures on the website.) Again, it's a small team, and while I would happily have someone of colour join the AB if they had the appropriate experience and knowledge, I would not proactively look for someone so that I could tick the diversity box. As you will know by now, I am not a box-ticking fan!

So, what do you think? Does our Advisory Board evidence that ORB is not a diverse organisation? I hope you agree that it is just not appropriate to use the constitution of our small AB as an indicator of our approach to diversity.

Chapter 8 The Environment

The environmental section embraces equally:

- Climate change
- Resource depletion
- Pollution, waste disposal
- Biodiversity loss

All businesses impact the above positively or negatively – most often both!

As with all sections in this book, I'm not suggesting that the information provided is finite in any shape or form. It is purely intended to provide touch points to get you thinking – and acting!

In recent years, general awareness of the global challenge of climate change has increased exponentially, yet an understanding of environmental and energy-related issues, and a commitment to make changes, have remained a comparatively low priority for many small businesses.

And yet suddenly, a move to net zero is the rallying call to avert disaster – and more small businesses than ever are stepping up to the challenge.

But as with the UN Sustainable Development Goals, we are not going to focus overtly on net zero for several reasons:

- As already mentioned, climate change is only one of the environmental impacts we need to consider

- A tick-box approach to net zero is inauthentic. Several companies are rushing to buy carbon credits to offset their emissions and claim to be net zero, but that is not an acceptable approach. Offsetting should only be used as a last resort to offset carbon emissions that are extremely difficult to avoid
- In the same vein, care must be taken to ensure that striving for net zero is embraced within a holistic approach to sustainable business that always considers the broader societal and environmental implications of our actions.
- By looking at all aspects of your business's environmental impacts and taking steps to reduce those impacts, you will automatically be working towards the ideal of net zero. For a small business, these are usually quite logical steps. Once you have taken appropriate action, then it is time to consider carbon footprint calculations and additional steps you may need to take to reach and, if you wish, certify to net zero.
- In other words, climate change is a big problem we all need to address as quickly as possible. Nonetheless, consider a more strategic option better suited to your business rather than a panicked approach. Investigate the environmental impacts of your business, not just a broad overview but by digging down into the detail of EVERY element of operations. Consider how you can improve and implement those steps urgently but in a logical progression.

Most small businesses can make these initial assessments and implement changes without additional and sometimes expensive expert advice or support. Additionally, there are often funded initiatives available to support micro and small businesses make environmental improvements, but these options frequently change and vary from area to area. Your local authority should be able to advise if there are any funding or support options available for your business.

If your authority has an Economic Development Department, they may also have a business database and even hold regular events for businesses. I recommend finding out and getting involved is one of the first steps you should take to ensure you do not miss out on environmental grants for businesses, with free training options and other local initiatives that could prove beneficial for your business.

Carbon Credits

As mentioned, purchasing carbon credits to offset emissions should only be considered as a last resort. But there are also innate issues with carbon credits that small businesses in particular need to be aware of.

For simplicity, I'll just talk about tree-planting as a trigger, I hope, to encourage you to thoroughly research your carbon offsetting – when you eventually get to that point.

Let me start by clarifying that this is not an anti-tree planting comment. I love trees. We have a comparatively small garden, albeit bigger than many, and have loads of trees, nearly all of which are indigenous and wildlife friendly.

And we do need to plant trees worldwide on a much bigger scale.

There are many excellent tree-planting schemes available, but some are also questionable because people have jumped on the tree-planting bandwagon as a business option to make money, or perhaps they just don't operate with the due diligence required for such projects. So, let's look at the bigger picture.

- There is not enough land on earth to plant enough trees to soak up all the carbon that big polluters are creating, so the priority must be changing habits and business models to reduce carbon emissions rather than resorting to tree-planting as a quick solution – 'cos it just isn't!
- Some tree-planting schemes are destroying the lands and livelihoods of indigenous peoples. At COP26, indigenous activists called carbon offset schemes 'a new form of colonialism'.
- Poorly planned and managed subsidies in some countries have encouraged the destruction of native forests, shrublands and grasslands to make way for monoculture plantations that have accelerated biodiversity loss and minimal overall carbon reduction.
- A newly-planted tree can take up to twenty years to capture the amount of CO_2 that a carbon offset scheme might promise.
- Thirty per cent of newly planted trees die within the first years of planting, primarily due to lack of care. If a local community is involved with the tree planting, that figure can be reduced to five per cent.
- Many scientists believe that planting trees on grasslands, peatlands or in tundra ecosystems can have unintended consequences that enhance warming.
- One of the most common statements when environmental experts discuss the merits and shortcomings of tree planting is that existing forests should never be cut down to plant new trees. Mature trees capture and store massive amounts of carbon and yet in comparison to tree planting, protecting forests has not received the attention it deserves.

If our priority must always be to nurture and protect existing forests and woodlands, how strange then that, according to the Forestry Commission, the amount of woodland in England managed sustainably has fallen by 40 per cent since 2014. Forty per cent in less than ten years at a time when we need to be maintaining our woodlands. How did that happen?

So, tree planting is good – if done correctly. Do your research.

No One Is Too Small to Make a Difference

Micro and small companies will often state that they are too small to make a difference, yet that is not the reality. Nearly six million enterprises in the UK employ less than ten people. If each of those small businesses only slightly reduces their environmental footprint, the overall impact will be huge.

Climate change is caused by the release of greenhouse gases into the atmosphere. While carbon dioxide is probably responsible for about two-thirds of anticipated global warming, other gases to consider are methane and nitrous oxide hydrofluorocarbons, perfluorocarbons and sulphur hexafluoride.

Many of our key business activities will cause the release of greenhouse gases, such as:

- Electricity and gas use
- Waste disposal and recycling
- Business travel, including the staff commute

Even seemingly 'innocent' aspects such as water usage (energy is needed to move and treat water) and internet usage have implications for carbon emissions.

Actually, that is rather an understatement.

Did you know that the carbon impact of the internet is greater than the aviation industry?

As Kayleigh Nicolaou explains:

A single search on Google emits between 0.2 and 7 grams of carbon dioxide. Visiting one web page with images or video emits around 0.2 grams a second, and an email is estimated to emit 4 grams of CO2. But, when you add a large attachment to an email, it can jump up to 50 grams of carbon dioxide emitted for a single email.

Those figures may seem small in isolation. But there are 40,000 Google searches every second, and 306.4 billion emails were sent daily in 2020. So, you can see that it quickly adds up to a massive amount of CO^2 released globally.

Shane Herath, founder of the Eco-Friendly Web Alliance, sums this up beautifully:

Perhaps because we cannot see the emissions caused by the web, we don't take it seriously as a contributor to global warming.

There's no smoke from the keyboards or chimneys attached to major data centres.

One of the first, easy steps you could take as a business is getting your website checked to see how carbon intensive it is. As Shane explains:

If you have a website which generates thousands of monthly page views, reducing the amount of energy consumed with each click can actually make a significant difference in lowering carbon emissions. Particularly as the global economy and society as a whole become increasingly digitised.

The internet accounts for 10 per cent of the world's electricity consumption. With life becoming more digitised all the time, and with developing countries catching up when it comes to internet use, consumption levels are going up dramatically and are likely to continue to do so.

Align Your Money With Your Values

Another aspect of business and private life that is commonly overlooked, and yet has colossal environmental and social implications, is where your money is invested. If you typically hold one thousand pounds or more in a current account, business or personal; or have a private pension plan; or operate or are a member of a workplace pension, this affects you. That probably includes a surprisingly large percentage of ordinary people reading this book.

Did you know that there is almost £3 trillion invested in UK pensions alone? Can you even begin to visualise how big that figure is? A large percentage of that money is undoubtedly driving deforestation and funding fossil fuels, tobacco, gambling and weapons. Some funds might be in accounts that have a 'do no harm' approach but consider the difference you could make if you pro-actively choose impact investments, a strategy that aims to generate positive social or environmental impacts in addition to financial gains. Many such ethical funds are now outperforming more traditional funds.

So do check your bank accounts, pensions, workplace pensions and any investments you might have and move your money so that it is supporting organisations and sectors aligned with your values.

* * *

As well as carbon emissions, there are numerous environmental consequences of our business operations. We all share these challenges and each of us has a responsibility to do what we can as individuals and as leaders of organisations. Yet the business advantages of doing so should not be overlooked.

Business Opportunities

Small businesses can transform environmental challenges into business opportunities, the most obvious of which is reducing overhead costs.

And it is not always necessary to make huge investments to start saving money.

We subscribe to the philosophy of eating the elephant in bite-sized chunks. Businesses can start by implementing low-cost and no-cost initiatives. If those savings are ring-fenced, investment in other environmental solutions can follow.

Apart from efficiency and cost savings, there may be other innovative business opportunities such as offering goods or services with reduced environmental impact in addition to those already provided; or, in certain instances, a completely new business model may evolve, e.g., a cleaning company offering an environmentally friendly service; a taxi company using only low emission and fuel-efficient vehicles.

There are also more specific opportunities in emerging eco-industries, including renewable technologies, which often attract substantial funding and support opportunities.

As with Health and Safety and Social Value, sound environmental practices are also invariably high on the list of requirements in both public and private sector contracts. It is therefore essential to demonstrate sound environmental management in your business if you wish to win more contracts.

Other customers are also impressed when companies can **authentically** evidence good environmental practices, as are graduates who may take this into consideration when assessing job opportunities. If you want to attract and retain the best staff, environmental responsibility is a key area.

Resource Efficiency

When thinking about environmental and energy-related issues, smaller businesses typically only think about recycling and reducing electricity and gas bills, but the agenda and, therefore, the potential benefits are much wider.

The Environment Agency estimates that being efficient with resources, including water, energy, packaging, transport, raw materials, and waste, can save UK companies billions of pounds each year, as well as helping to streamline operations.

The Bigger Picture

In the Western world, we use far more resources than we can produce, creating long-term challenges.

It is suggested that if everyone lived in the same manner as they do in the US, we would need four Earths to support us.

Fortunately, an increasing percentage of people in the Western world are now conscious of reducing their environmental impacts. Conversely, their environmental impacts will significantly increase as developing countries evolve with aspirations for a 'better' lifestyle.

As COP 26 evidenced so clearly, the developed nations have caused the bulk of climate change issues, yet the poorer, underdeveloped nations are most affected. For those countries, it is not about challenges they are facing in the future – climate change is affecting them NOW!

Can we really maintain a 'business as usual' mentality and ignore the dire results of a greed-driven capitalist society that values profits more than anything else?

The concept of finite resources is not one that resonates with us in the UK. We are used to a world of plenty where we have access to anything we need, whenever we want it, apart from extraordinary circumstances such as the pandemic and Brexit. Together with the intrinsic problems associated with our dependence on imports, often from unstable countries, considering resource efficiency is an absolute necessity. But as we struggle to reduce our dependency on fossil fuels and generally reduce our environmental impact, our choices can sometimes be far-reaching, complex and confusing.

As already mentioned, continuing devastation of essential rainforests is an immediate example. We can help by ensuring we purchase wood and wood products that are FSC (Forest Stewardship Council) or similarly certified. Paper used should have appropriate certification (albeit there can be a confusing array) or recycled.

Another example is early forays in the development of first-generation biofuels. The intention of providing an alternative to fossil fuels seemed an honourable one. Yet, those first solutions ignored the fact that land used to grow fuel crops had previously been used to support the livelihoods of indigenous communities in third-world countries. Sadly, the impact on those communities was devastating.

Too many communities in the developing world already live in abject poverty without access to the basic human needs of sufficient food, water, sanitation, education, shelter and clothing. We must always ask ourselves if our actions will help other communities improve their lives or add to their deprivations.

We must strive to make decisions based on a holistic viewpoint that considers the local environment, the wider environment and most importantly, communities worldwide that may be negatively impacted by our sometimes rather short-sighted albeit well-intentioned actions.

Fortunately, advanced biofuels are now far more diverse in their origins, and a more sustainable approach to creation and production has been adopted.

Waste

All businesses have a legal duty to prevent waste and to apply the waste hierarchy.

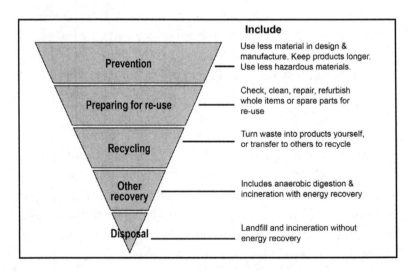

Even small businesses must meet legislative requirements when disposing of waste, such as handling and storing waste appropriately, particularly hazardous waste; ensuring waste carriers are licensed; obtaining and retaining waste transfer notes; and meeting WEEE legislation (waste electrical and electronic equipment recycling).

E-waste is a particularly sensitive issue as the equipment typically contains rare earth metals, some of which are very toxic. Do make sure IT equipment is collected by a specialist company that can also ensure all data is properly wiped from the machine and that they supply you with appropriate documentation.

Such companies may also refurbish electronic equipment and make it available for schools or charities either free of charge or at significantly reduced rates.

Apart from a legal duty, reducing waste can have a significant positive impact on the bottom line, an aspect many businesses underestimate.

But before thinking about how to dispose of e-waste, consider if you really need to buy new electrical or electronic equipment. Rather than new, is repair or an upgrade available, or perhaps refurbished equipment would suffice? Although a small item, a significant example is mobile phones, as most providers aggressively encourage upgrades to a new model as soon as one contract ends. If your current mobile does the job, don't be tempted to upgrade to a newer model just because it has an additional widget that you may not even use.

The world is estimated to produce around 50 million metric tons of e-waste annually. Around 10 per cent of the total is made up of small electronics like smartphones, and that percentage is expected to continue rising.

As raw material costs continue to rise, particularly for those substances where security of supply is questionable due to physical and geopolitical risks, reducing waste will be an increasingly critical issue for all businesses. Reducing the volume of products and raw materials used might involve re-assessing design and manufacturing processes. Taking appropriate action may well result in surprising efficiencies and cost savings.

But even if you are a tiny business and just cut down on stationery usage, you will be making a small difference and avoiding the costs of excessive stock sitting in your stationery cupboard. Don't be tempted by the seemingly excellent savings of buying printed stationery in bulk. I did just that. I still use complimentary slips for to-do lists and shopping lists many years later. Unless you are sure you will use large quantities of stationery, bulk purchasers are a false economy for your pocket and the environment.

Many items can be re-used as per my now scrap paper for notes. Or it could be shredded and used as packaging material. But clearly, it's best to reduce first rather than re-use.

Larger items can often be repaired or refurbished as complete items or spares. If you cannot re-use, recycling is the next option.

Do you know what your licensed carrier does with your waste? Is as much as possible recycled, or is it all going to landfill?

Hazardous substances should not be included with general waste. Waste transfer notes for hazardous substances should be kept for three years and include a 'Consignee's Return to a Producer or Holder' document, returned to you no later than four months after the waste has left your site, which confirms what has been done with the waste.

Note that hazardous substances include substances you may not have realised fit this category. One of the most common substances not dealt with adequately are cleaning materials such as bleach, sanitisers and toilet cleaners. If possible, change to environmentally friendly alternatives. If this is not possible, ensure you are compliant.

Other 'hazardous' items you may not have considered include but are not limited to electrical and electronic equipment such as TVs, computer monitors, printer cartridges, fridges, fluorescent lighting, solvent-based paint, engine oils, lead-acid batteries and essential oils.

And do not forget that one man's waste can be another's raw material. Certain waste streams can sometimes be sold as opposed to being sent to landfill at a cost, resulting in increased profitability through reduced costs and increased sales.

Appropriately disposing of waste can be challenging for many small businesses because of the lack of available facilities. If you are in this situation, consider how you might be able to work with other local businesses to share waste facilities.

Water as a readily available resource is under threat in the driest areas of the UK, and increasingly more regions will be impacted as climate change results in longer, drier periods right across the country. Yet frequently, little thought is given to its usage. Businesses pay for both water supply and water disposal;

implementing simple and inexpensive ways of minimising water usages, such as good maintenance and fitting water-minimising controls, could halve their water costs.

You will need appropriate authorisation and permits if you have any discharges to surface and ground waters other than uncontaminated water. Similarly, besides clean, uncontaminated water and sewage from domestic facilities, you must not discharge any other trade effluent to a public foul sewer without appropriate consents.

Energy

There are many ways to reduce energy consumption, from no and low-cost options to larger projects involving considerable capital outlay. Such projects could relate directly to energy costs and production, such as solar installations, or indirectly such as more energy-efficient equipment and machinery – which invariably also reduces production times.

Before embarking on any large project, it will be important to check the ROI (return on investment). The natural laws of supply and demand, fortunately, mean that costs for energy-efficient investments are continually falling. Additionally, as I have already mentioned, there are schemes available that may part-fund new equipment that offers a considerable reduction in environmental impacts.

Thought should also be given to energy supplies from energy companies: most offer renewable options.

Supply Chain

Consider how you can influence your suppliers to be more environmentally conscious and purchase sustainable goods and services whenever possible.

Transportation

Transportation has a significant impact on the local environment as well as contributing to global climate change. Consider not only the transport used directly in your business but also inward transportation of goods and how staff travel to work.

Using public transport and offering work-from-home options as appropriate can have significant impacts.

In terms of cars used for business purposes, it does not matter if they are company owned or owned by individuals; if used for company purposes, their impact should be considered (those cars should also be insured for business use and records kept to ensure they are MOT'd and serviced).

Many companies are now changing to electric or alternative fuel vehicles. However, if annual mileage is extremely low and your vehicle is reasonably fuel-efficient, and you do not really need a new car, do remember that every new vehicle has enormous amounts of embodied carbon, i.e. the total emissions that result from its production. It is estimated that a small electric car has about 14 tonnes of CO_2e. The larger the vehicle, the larger the embodied carbon.

Currently, the energy used to build most new cars will come from burning fossil fuels. Batteries are currently carbon-intensive to manufacture. As manufacturing processes change and larger companies focus on net zero plants, embodied carbon in electric cars and other products will reduce dramatically. So, if you are in that low mileage bracket and do not need a new car now, it makes sense to wait a couple of years before swapping it in for an electric vehicle.

Decisions are not always straightforward, are they?

Getting Started

As small businesses are so vastly different, there is no one-size-fits-all benchmark for environmental performance nor a comprehensive list of actions to take and solutions offered. Indeed, small businesses may be severely restricted in the actions they can implement if, for example, they are in serviced offices that have not embraced environmental considerations. In such instances, business owners must do as much as they can internally and try to encourage the property owners to embrace resource efficiency and carbon reduction initiatives.

What is most important is that businesses assess their environmental impacts, however small they may be, and implement a plan to start reducing them.

To assess your impacts, you really need to carry out an audit, but you can do this easily yourself or use an external environmental consultant for a 'walk-round' audit. This should not be expensive, and in certain areas funding is in place for free audits. Being clear on your existing impacts and the various options to save money, often at low or no cost, will certainly be worth the effort.

Draft a policy statement to show your intent. It should be concise and no more than one side of A4. A few short paragraphs are generally sufficient for a micro business.

You might then consider implementing an environmental management system (EMS) – but don't panic. This, too, can be surprisingly simple. An EMS is a systematic way of managing all immediate and long-term environmental aspects of an organisation's premises and operations, typically including energy efficiency, material efficiency, waste and water. It may also include biodiversity, although this is usually inappropriate for most small businesses.

An EMS should generally be written, be used and understood throughout the company, and focus on continual improvement of the system. An EMS does not have to be ISO 14001. If you are a one-man band web designer working from a home office, you could still implement an EMS, even if it is only a couple of paragraphs.

You have an environmental policy; you have identified the impacts. Assuming, of course, you are meeting environmental legislation; there are now four key steps:

- Set a plan to implement improvements (everything does not have to be done immediately).
- Ensure procedures are in place for day-to-day environmental actions, and everyone understands those processes and their specific responsibilities.
- Continually monitor and measure impacts.
- Review plans and procedures regularly to ensure continual improvement.

If you have staff, ensuring they are all engaged in your environmental aspirations will help to embed any changes. And do not discount employees working from home. It may even be appropriate to consider an 'environmental champion' who can encourage their peers to buy into relevant environmental initiatives that are launched.

Environmental Conservation

You might also consider the morale-boosting benefits of proactively engaging in environmental conservation projects. Examples could be active membership of a wildlife trust, especially if that includes volunteering at nature reserves, providing nesting boxes for bats or birds, introducing planters with bee-friendly flowers, or a grow-your-own project if you have the space.

The Built Environment

The built environment plays such a huge role in the social and environmental agenda that it is worth a specific mention. New developments now require high environmental standards and there are also an increasing number of retrofit projects. Quality of life should always be a consideration in these projects: while the key priority may be a reduction in environmental impact in both the embedded carbon in construction materials used and reductions in ongoing energy consumption, the social implications in terms of producing those products (e.g. child labour in brick making in India) and the quality of life of the inhabitants of those domestic and commercial dwellings (e.g. fresh air, warmth, water, light and natural environment) should not be underestimated.

There are thousands of small businesses, including sole proprietors involved in the construction industry, who do not have the necessary knowledge and skills that would enable them to offer innovative and environmentally focused technologies, products and services. This can create a challenge as the time and financial costs involved in extensive re-training can be prohibitive. However, the Supply Chain Sustainability School provides a free online learning environment to help construction suppliers and sub-contractors develop their sustainability knowledge and competence.

We strongly recommend this excellent initiative is used by all small businesses in the construction industry as part of their ongoing training and development plans if they wish to retain and indeed increase their competitive advantage. The tool is entirely confidential and provides access to free resources, including the ability to develop personalised action plans.

Chapter 9 Customers and Suppliers

Excellent Relationships

Excellent relationships with customers and suppliers that continually build on a rock-solid reputation are the bedrock of good business. Such relationships can only be forged if staff are appropriately trained, happy, engaged and motivated, as this will reflect in their dealings with customers and suppliers.

Delighting the Customer

Of course, there also needs to be a business commitment to ethical and professional standards, and systems and processes must be in place to ensure the customer is always delighted.

But although the goal is to get it right first time, mistakes will happen, and a company is often judged more on its ability to deal with issues than on a straightforward supply. Clear customer information, complete transparency and efficient complaints procedures are vital.

Ensuring staff are adequately trained to deal with complaint handling is particularly important. The ability to be empathetic and yet remain efficient with unhappy customers is a quality not to be overlooked.

> Do what you do so well and so uniquely that people cannot resist telling others about you.

Walt Disney

Consider how you delight your customer with your goods and services. What systems do you have in place to ensure goods are fit for purpose? Do you have a documented system if you are providing a service to ensure you have fully understood your client's requirements? Are you totally honest and transparent, ensuring goods are appropriately labelled and terms and conditions, including guarantees, warranties, and returns policies, are clear?

Vulnerable Customers

Organisations may have customers or potential customers who are vulnerable. Every effort should be made to provide them with a service adequate for their needs and make special provisions as appropriate.

If direct services are provided to children, young people or vulnerable adults, Safeguarding Policies must be in place, staff must have adequate training and DBS (Disclosure and Barring Service) checks should be conducted as appropriate.

Getting Feedback

The only way you can truly know if you are delighting your customers is by ensuring you get feedback, good and bad, as quickly as possible – and act on the results. Trust Pilot and similar services are used in many sectors, but one always wonders if the comments are all 100 per cent genuine. You may be in a sector, such as the hospitality industry, where this type of third-party review is the norm, and then, of course, it makes sense to use that system. But direct questions with responses back to your company are going to be a far more accurate gauge as to whether or not you got it right. This should be an automatic aspect of your after-sales care.

So much of the above is common sense, and yet it is easy for standards to slip, particularly if training, good communication and workplace culture are not continually reviewed and maintained to the highest possible levels.

There is also a great deal of legislation intended to protect the customer, including but certainly not limited to the Green Claims Code, which we have already touched upon. Trading Standards have a website that provides free, impartial legal guidance for businesses (see resource section at the end of the book). Even the GOV.UK website has comprehensive information on a range of topics.

As the saying goes: 'You don't know what you don't know.'

Unless you are a member of a specific sector body that can provide appropriate information, checking out the Business Companion website developed by Trading Standards is recommended to ensure you are not inadvertently falling foul of any legislation (see resources at the end of the book).

Consider, too, what insurances you need. The only insurances you are legally required to have are Employer's Liability Insurance and vehicle insurance as appropriate. But it is a very foolhardy and irresponsible business that does not consider other insurances. You'll probably need general insurance to protect your business assets, but you also may need to consider Public Liability Insurance and Professional Indemnity Insurance. The former is a must if you deal with the general public in any way whatsoever, whereas the latter mainly applies to businesses providing professional advice. Consider, for example, if you are a healthcare professional and you provide advice that proves to be negligent or a solicitor that provides advice that results in a significant financial loss. No one wants to be in that position, but should the worst happen, the impact can be catastrophic for the business if appropriate insurance is not in place. It could also be disastrous for the customer if they are facing the consequences of poor advice and the process for them to obtain appropriate recourse is made more challenging because no insurance is in place.

If you have PI insurance and you use freelancers, do consider how that affects your insurance. If a claim is made on your insurance and a freelancer has carried out the work in question on your behalf, and they do not have their own insurance, your insurance company may not pay out unless specified in the terms and conditions.

Seek professional advice if you are unsure if professional liability is essential or advisable for your business.

And be aware that working from home without informing your insurers could invalidate a standard domestic insurance policy.

In addition to considering how you delight the customer, do also consider how the customer treats you, their supplier.

This is particularly pertinent when a small business wins a juicy contract with a big company. Initially, the champagne corks may be popping to celebrate winning such a big contract. But a few months later, you may need someone to wipe your tears. Why? Because you may have created a major cash flow issue for yourself!

Turnover Is Vanity, Profit Is Sanity, but Cashflow Is King

As any accountant will tell you, businesses who ignore this phrase do so at their peril.

Liz Barclay, the Small Business Commissioner for the UK, is working hard to change the culture of poor payment practices. She says that:

Small firms should be treated with respect by their bigger customers and paid on time and fairly, without having to agree to wait months for payment or forgo the contract.

She adds that small businesses are vital because:

They keep the country going. And after the bad times, they are first back to the drawing board, starting again and rebuilding the economy. They deserve respect and support and to be treated fairly by their bigger customers. And that means fair contracts, with fair payment terms, and processes that get the money they're owed to them as quickly as technology allows so that they can get on with supplying the next order, innovating, and growing, creating jobs along the way.

Non-payment, late payment or unfair payment terms create real uncertainty. Suppliers lie awake at night, and ultimately, there's a threat to the existence of the business. That can impact badly on mental health and the family and home. Getting paid on time can be the difference between feeding your children over the weekend or them going hungry.

If this sounds rather extreme, Liz and her team can assure you that they repeatedly deal with business owners in these extreme situations because of bad payment practices by their bigger clients.

But Liz also stresses that while the commission is working hard to improve payment practices, small businesses need to ensure that they NEVER accept a contract if payment terms are more than 60 days. Ideally, payment terms should be 30 days or less. Her team has experienced far too many cases where payment terms in a contract are 90, 120 or even 180 days, and the small business is unaware of what they have agreed to because they have not 'read the small print.'

If a small company has not been paid within agreed terms, it is generally comparatively easy for the Small Business Commission to ensure this is rectified quite quickly. However, if a big company is not breaching contract terms, while the commission can provide a certain amount of light touch pressure, they certainly would not be able to guarantee the desired result of early payment.

And so, be very wary if you are doing business with a big business customer. Sadly, if their ethics and values do not match yours, what appears to be a lucrative and profitable contract could turn into the worst business decision you have ever made. Your worst nightmare could be looming...

CASE STUDY

Mike Jennings, Chairman of the Jennings Group and author of *Valuable: How a Values-Enabled Culture Can Inspire You to Sustainable Profit*, takes a very different approach with his customers.

Valuable is a true story, Mike's personal story, and the philosophy of putting trust at the heart of your business.

Mike's grandfather bought a farm in Oxfordshire in the 1920s which, with a few changes along the way, was predominantly a poultry farm. Later, another site was purchased and then in the 1970s, with the new large supermarkets imposing their purchasing power on farmers,

Mike's father and uncle started to convert farm buildings into workshops, a common site across the UK.

Mike went to university and then followed a route in the accountancy profession. But eventually, he returned to 'the farm' to help his father with what was by then a small business park. He began by introducing appropriate systems to increase operational efficiencies. Nonetheless, carrying on the tradition that his father had already established and that aligned with his innate desire to build good relationships, Mike ensured from the outset that he made and maintained excellent relationships with his customers, the workshop tenants, based on trust and mutual respect.

Mike's father died suddenly in 1995, and Mike took on board the responsibility for managing and developing the business. That never diminished Mike's determination to build a business community where people felt valued, and the small businesses were supported. To this day, Jennings' mission is:

To create a positive impact on the economy, environment, and society through the support we provide for businesses and people.

The business has grown and now includes business units, service offices, meeting rooms, hot desks, containers and storage, and so much more.

But rather like the example of our young man with his cleaning business, Mike did not follow the typical landlord/

tenant route of complex leases with lengthy tie-ins, dilapidation clauses and a multitude of complexities.

Easy in and out options are now quite commonplace for office units, but they certainly were not all those years ago and are still not for business units and workshops.

But Mike took a route based on mutual trust. While he is the first to admit that this has been abused on rare occasions, in the main, this has created an excellent working environment for all concerned, reflected in a profitable, successful business. A business that continually gives back.

Jennings doesn't use a solicitor to write complex leases. Their four-page version unambiguously states expectations on both sides, thus avoiding contractual complications. Tenants can stay as long as they want and leave at short notice. Rent reviews will be conducted with a chat over a cup of coffee.

If tenants are struggling, they know they can talk to the Jennings team, who will aim to help perhaps with a rent holiday, by allowing them to sublet or moving them to a smaller unit.

If tenants want to make changes to a unit, they can ask, and permission is rarely refused, subject to the proviso that it may be necessary to reverse the changes when they leave.

It is a rarity that tenants are asked to pay for dilapidations. The requirement is for tenants to leave the unit tidy, sweep up after themselves and pay a small fee for redecoration costs.

Being kind and considerate does not mean that Mike or his team are a 'soft touch'. And indeed, when the rare occasion arises where it is essential to exert their authority as landlords, they do so swiftly, fairly and professionally.

As Mike says:

Fulfilment in business comes not from maximising profit but from the human interaction of daily life.

* * *

And as we say:

DOING GOOD IS GOOD FOR BUSINESS

Suppliers as Business Partners

People often forget the importance of building good relationships with their suppliers. They should be treated with the same level of respect as customers. If suppliers are considered business partners, a mutually beneficial relationship will evolve.

Suppliers have a wealth of information about their products and services, the latest trends and technologies, and exclusive offers and promotions. Most importantly, building those relationships with your suppliers will help to ensure the quality of the goods and services provided, continuity of supply, and responsiveness to special requests when required.

It Really Is Just Good Business

Meeting payment terms is a crucial aspect of building such relationships. Adopting a policy of paying all invoices in 30 days as a maximum should be a given. After all, if we expect our clients to pay us in a timely fashion, we should also extend that courtesy to our suppliers.

If you have a good relationship with your suppliers and usually pay promptly, should you experience cash flow issues, negotiating an extended payment period, if necessary, will be managed far more easily if a relationship based on mutual trust and respect is already in place. Once again, communication comes to the fore. Rather than digging your head in the sand if cash flow problems loom, assess the situation as soon as possible and make a realistic schedule of how you can manage payment of outstanding invoices and then speak with your suppliers. Be honest, it's the best policy, and invariably you'll be able to work through the challenging period together.

Fair and Ethical Purchasing

We should treat our direct suppliers fairly and consider committing to a fair and ethical purchasing policy so that suppliers, however far down the chain, adhere to a code of fair and ethical labour practice. This would ensure fair wages, hours of work, safe and hygienic working conditions, a fair price for producers that covers the total cost of production and enables a living wage, and no child labour.

For some businesses, this might be particularly hard to monitor, but an awareness of such issues and a commitment to withdraw products if unjust labour policies exist may suffice. In such instances, a fair and ethical purchasing policy could state that the company never knowingly sells products produced using unethical labour practices.

168

Proactively sourcing Fair Trade alternatives, when possible, could help to mitigate the inability to have complete control.

Most importantly, statements that cannot possibly be accurate should never be made, so ultimately, it will be better not to have a policy than to be 'greenwashing'. i.e. Making statements that do not stand up to scrutiny.

Bribery and Corruption

Bribery and corruption are rife, particularly in developing countries, and can fuel the deprivation of the poorest communities.

Bribery and corruption policies should be in place *where appropriate*, particularly where any trading overseas is involved.

Did you know that under the Bribery Act 2010, if an agent, subsidiary or other person performing services for your business commits a general bribery offence, the company and the directors could be found guilty of an offence if adequate precautions to prevent bribery are not in place? The penalties can be severe, including possible custodial sentences.

If you are in an industry with a large and complex supply chain, you may want to consider registering with a company such as SEDEX to manage your supply chain risk and positively impact workers in your global supply chain.

Chapter 10 The Community

Today's society faces many social challenges, and unless you work on an island, you will no doubt be aware of some of the challenges in your local community.

Poverty, hunger, abuse, mental illness, physical illness, homelessness, addiction, lack of aspiration, lack of opportunity, loneliness, and modern-day slavery. None of this is new. Shocking inequalities are often very close, even for those living comfortably in leafy suburbs. For example, I live in Southend-on-Sea, and there is a 10-year disparity in life expectancy between two adjacent wards. This is a common story.

We are all impacted by the health and vibrancy of our local community, either directly or indirectly. As business owners, understanding the problems in our local community and providing support in a way that is appropriate for us and appropriate for the community we serve should be a given.

A desire to support the local community is not only the morally correct approach to take, but proactively getting involved is also good for business.

However, it is important to stress that if you are considering community engagement projects purely for business benefit, this will not go unnoticed by either staff or the community. If your approach lacks authenticity, you could be accused of 'greenwashing' and all the potential benefits negated.

A wise business nurtures its local community so that both thrive together.

While some might consider this onerous, time-consuming or expensive, engaging with and supporting the local community should be considered an extremely rewarding business opportunity.

Community involvement can have the bonus of not only enhancing your business's reputation and therefore helping to increase turnover, but it is also excellent for increasing staff morale and retention.

Invariably, there will also be publicity opportunities. Charities are particularly good at ensuring their business supporters receive press coverage. There may also be local award opportunities.

Let's look at some of the benefits:

- Enhanced reputation and competitive advantage
- Reduced risk
- Becoming an employer of choice
- Excellent marketing opportunities
- Increased staff engagement and motivation
- Helping you win public and private contracts
- Inspiring innovation and increased business opportunities
- Gaining new skills
- You'll feel good too!

A Small Budget

Big corporations often have huge budgets for community projects, but small businesses can engage for minimal cost.

It makes commercial sense to offer something relating to your business. For example, a first-aid training company might offer free first-aid classes to new mums, or a web developer may design a website for a new charity or community group. But ultimately, the type of involvement will vary greatly according to the company's main characteristics, senior management's particular interests, and any specific requests from staff.

If you are struggling to drive any community projects within the business, you might like to enlist the help and support of an enthusiastic staff member. There may also be organisations in your area that help businesses and charities connect.

What Kind of Activities?

Why not brainstorm with your staff to develop a 12-month community engagement programme? Don't make it too ambitious to start with. The following are a few ideas, but with a bit of enthusiasm and initiative, the possibilities become endless:

- Fundraise for your charity of the year: fun runs, bike rides, tombolo, etc.
- Provide the 'strip' for a children's sports team
- Initiate staff volunteering schemes
- Sponsor local events
- Donate products or prizes to local charities
- Partner with a local school or college and offer mentoring support
- Offer work experience or apprenticeship opportunities
- Offer heavily discounted or pro-bono services to local charities
- Take part in local environmental schemes
- Get involved in local business forums
- Payroll Giving Schemes
- Become a trustee of a charity, or a school governor

Projects may become available on an ad hoc basis, such as a local group wanting to build a community garden. If you are involved and building extensive local networks, you are more likely to hear about innovative projects that will inspire staff.

Supporting Youth Employment

Perhaps one of the best ways a company can support their community is to offer mentoring, work experience placements or take on apprentices.

This approach can also be extended to other groups with barriers to employment, such as those with disabilities, homeless, or with criminal records. If offering work opportunities is too challenging, and unquestionably not everybody is in a position to do so, mentoring people who often have extremely low confidence and aspirations can be incredibly rewarding.

There would be no youth unemployment if 1 in 4 SMEs were to take on a young person.

Research shows that a young person with four or more encounters with employers is 86 per cent less likely to be unemployed or not in education or training and can earn up to 18 per cent more during their career.

Collaborating with schools offers the chance to inspire young people to consider a career in your industry or company. Importantly, a strong school-business collaboration is far more than just a healthy talent pipeline for the future. Such programmes are highly motivating for employees acting as mentors who will often learn new, transferrable skills. They can also lead to proud, loyal employees, more trusting customers and enthusiastic company advocates.

Rather than approaching a school or college direct, it is invariably better, if possible, to join an existing mentoring scheme. Contact your local authority, who should be able to advise on opportunities available.

Philanthropy

Technically, philanthropy can also refer to charitable acts or other good works. Personally, I prefer to differentiate between philanthropic financial donations and the broader aspect of supporting the local community.

There is nothing wrong with philanthropy providing it is not approached as a means of 'purchasing' one's ethical and social badge.

Naturally, if an individual or a company is financially able to do so, charitable donations are needed more than ever to help the post-COVID-19 recovery and a cost-of-living crisis that seems remorseless.

Focusing on genuine community engagement rather than *just* financial giving is considerably more rewarding for all concerned. There may be situations where involvement is difficult, and philanthropy provides the solution. Alternatively, a generous donation of money to good causes given alongside more proactive community involvement can provide the best possible outcomes.

As mentioned in an earlier chapter, businesses may also wish to consider adopting cause marketing strategies alongside other aspects of community engagement.

To reiterate, cause marketing is when a business publicly pledges to donate to charity, directly linked to sales or turnover of their goods or services. This could be an overall percentage or a more specific amount. For example: 'We will donate £5 for each t-shirt sold in June 2023 to XX charity.'

This is a win-win as the business will raise its profile and potentially increase sales while raising money for a good cause.

The Responsible Business Standard certification process treats philanthropy as a separate question. And because we would not necessarily expect philanthropic donations in addition to actual community involvement, this section can be marked as not applicable without a detrimental impact on scoring. This approach rubber stamps our assertions that genuine community support is not something that can be bought.

Local People and Local Sourcing

I have already mentioned the importance of supporting young people or any other group furthest from the labour market. Employing local people as much as possible is equally important.

Local sourcing is also essential. Just as we always encourage consumers to 'buy local' and support their high streets, businesses should unite to support each other and keep money in the local economy. This also allows for much stronger relationships to be developed, plus, generally, there are additional environmental benefits. That will never be possible for all goods and services but checking what you can get locally before you go further afield is important.

Of course, it is essential not to buy local at the expense of other important factors such as cost and quality and the social and environmental attributes you would expect from any supplier.

Chapter 11 Communicating Values Internally and Externally

Throughout this book, I have spoken a great deal about the importance of good communication, but I think it is worth 'pulling it all together', hence a brief recap on how you communicate your values.

In the Responsible Business Standard certification, one of the sections is called Ethics, Values and Transparency. These attributes should be at the heart of an organisation and therefore intrinsically embedded in all the other sections of the certification process. But the reason we have a separate section is to ascertain how those attributes are being communicated internally and externally. And from personal experience, very few micro and small companies are doing that effectively.

So, let's start at the beginning!

What are the values that underpin your business? Can you articulate them immediately? Could the rest of your team? Are they written down anywhere?

If you can't answer all four questions immediately, you've got some work to do!

As shown in his case study, Mike Jennings adopted a values-based approach to his business from the beginning. But they were his values. His way of treating his people. His way of treating his tenants. As the business and his team grew, Mike realised that his team did not always understand his approach. He wanted his people to embrace the values he held dear but sometimes struggled to contextualise and verbalise those values effectively in the business context.

He set aside two days to work with his Business Park Manager and his trusted Business Coach to brainstorm what those values, together with explanatory straplines, should be. The result reflected what they were already doing and set a standard of aspirational behaviours that the team could embrace.

The following are the Jennings company values which seem both generic in terms of values that everyone could and should adopt and yet specific in that they are pertinent to the operation of a business park.

- **Openness and Honesty**: for the sake of minimising the fears and anxieties associated with renting premises.
- **Accommodating**: for the sake of making people feel at home.
- **Commitment**: for the sake of delivering a service that exceeds expectations.
- **Fairness**: for the sake of establishing loyalty and trust.
- **Courtesy**: for the sake of creating an environment where people feel valued.
- **Trust**: for the sake of enabling relationships to grow.

The way these values are framed creates a reference point that the team can refer to if they are unsure how to react in any given situation by simply prefacing the strapline with 'how will this.'

For example:

How will this establish loyalty and trust?

How will this create an environment where people feel valued?

If you have not yet identified and written down your company values, I suggest this is an excellent approach.

But just writing this down is not enough. The values you have established need to be shared. They need to be discussed. They need to be embedded throughout the company. And they should be shared externally as well as internally.

And even more importantly, you need to lead by example. And if you make a mistake, have the courage to admit you've messed up. None of us is perfect, but no one can expect their people to live the company values if the boss doesn't do so. That's one of the reasons why CSR or ESG can seem so hollow in large businesses – because putting people and the environment before profit is rarely a philosophy adopted by senior executives.

A good way of sharing the company values, code of ethics, mission and vision, etc., is via the company website. But I've lost count of the number of websites that contain the standard rhetoric: how many years of experience the team has between them, the fantastic service they provide, and the wonderful products and services they offer. That alone is going to sound more like a sales page.

What does the About Us page on your website say about your company, you, and your team? What does it tell your potential clients?

Of course, your customers want to know they will get great products and services and fantastic customer care, but they also want to know they are buying from people they like and trust.

The About Us page should focus on building trust and encouraging your customers to *invest emotionally* in your brand. What is it that makes your brand, you and your team unique?

By all means, have a team section, but a list of names and job roles, even if a picture is included, isn't going to rock anyone's boat. Make it personal. Yes, education, experience, and expertise are all important, but where's the human factor? Does the founder take her dog to work? Does Jo, in accounts, love spending the weekend on her allotment? Is Tom, head of marketing, learning how to play the guitar? If those profiles can include anything relating to caring about people and the environment, that's great. But don't over-egg it. It must be authentic.

Do you have a story to tell? This can be a powerful way of building trust. Seffie Wells tells her story of fleeing her home with her newborn from domestic abuse. Mitali tells the story of being a ghost-writer for high-level business leaders and entrepreneurs before becoming disillusioned and launching her own business so she could work only with ethical and responsible businesses (and no, in case you are suddenly wondering, I have not used a ghost-writer. I have blundered through the initial writing of this book on my own!).

Highlighting company values should be a key element of the About Us section but extend that as appropriate to include aspects of how you support your people, your local community and your approach to sustainability.

And naturally, if you are a member of the Organisation for Responsible Businesses, have Investors in People accreditation, are signed up to the Prompt Payment Code, achieved net zero or Carbon Positive certification, Responsible Business Standard certification or anything similar, do ensure you display the correct logos on your website but, as already mentioned, only if the membership or certification has genuine value.

But always, always, always – be authentic!

One of the applicants for our Business and Community Charter Award was able to immediately evidence what they were doing in the community by signposting us to their community page on their website, which highlighted all the activities they had been involved with throughout the year. It was a real pleasure looking through their community section and seeing all the pictures of happy directors, managers and staff getting involved in what were sometimes quite weird and wonderful fundraising events!

As well as adding such events and achievements to your website, share your achievements with your people and on social media.

To reiterate, if robust, successful, profitable businesses are talking about the good things they are doing, it becomes the norm rather than something that 'those tree hugger types do!'

Share the message loud and clear.

* * *

DOING GOOD IS GOOD FOR BUSINESS

* * *

Don't forget the importance of ensuring any sub-contractors and suppliers are also aware of your values and that you are not prepared for those values to be compromised by the goods and services they are providing.

And consider what you can do to promote the principles of responsible business with other businesses or business organisations. Have those conversations. Encourage others to get involved. Engaging with sector-specific organisations to share, promote and support general business development and the broader responsible business movement can be very rewarding and earn you a great deal of respect.

Chapter 12 Business Processes and Business Continuity

These topics, particularly business processes, are covered in thousands of books. It's a huge topic. But don't worry – this section is a quite light touch.

You might even wonder why I have included it in this book about responsible business. Where does that fit in?

I'll remind you, if I may, of ORB's definition of responsible business:

> A responsible business operates efficiently and ethically, meets and exceeds legislation, and always considers its impact on people (the workforce, the community, society at large), and the environment.

There it is, in the very first sentence. **A responsible business operates efficiently**...

Having appropriate business policies, procedures and systems in place is essential to running even the smallest business efficiently, but the complexities will vary greatly. A sole proprietor may have very little written down, whereas a larger food manufacturer may have extensive documentation. But even, for example, a sole proprietor needs to ensure he is looking at the most recent version of a document.

It is also essential that individuals are very clear on their roles. In a small company, it is common for employees to have numerous responsibilities. The danger is that unless roles are well-defined, certain processes can be missed entirely if staff are absent. A list of job functions, who has primary responsibility for them, and who is capable of covering them is essential.

Business continuity is another area that is often given little thought. And while no one could have foreseen the chaos brought about by the pandemic and successive lockdowns in 2020 and 2021, organisations with business continuity policies and processes fared much better than those without.

Sadly, even before the pandemic, many good businesses have encountered an unforeseen disaster, such as a major fire, IT system failure, or sudden illness or death of key personnel, and have been unable to recover.

Adequate insurance will undoubtedly help in such situations, but it can never replace the potential loss of goodwill and subsequent loss of customers. Good planning can help businesses to minimise the risks and withstand the impacts of such disasters.

Don't let chaos envelop your business purely because you do not have an adequate business continuity plan to minimise the risks and withstand the impacts of potential disasters.

There are many BCP experts around, and you will also find templates to download if you search the internet. But you and your team should be able to do most of the work yourselves. Have a brainstorming session and invite your people to consider unforeseen events that could seriously impact your business, with the proviso that all worst-case scenarios should be thrown into the melting pot, however bizarre they may seem.

There are five critical components of a business continuity plan:

1. Identify the risks and the potential business impact
2. Identify the steps needed to a) minimise the likelihood of the risk, such as comprehensive maintenance agreements that include emergency call-outs for vital equipment; and b) the response to be taken if the risk arises
3. Document the roles and responsibilities
4. Communication is vital both internally and externally. Ensure a key list of contacts is accessible, including insurers and service providers and, as appropriate, prepare templated press and social media posts
5. Train your people and test the effectiveness of the plans

The first hour after an emergency is often the most critical. It is essential to determine what key business functions need to be operational first, and all staff should know and understand their respective roles in an emergency.

Adequate business interruption (BI) insurance will undoubtedly help in many instances, but it can never replace the potential loss of goodwill and subsequent loss of customers. And if you do have BI, read the small print carefully. While the insurance industry is now expected to pay up to £2bn in business interruption COVID claims incurred during 2020 following the Supreme Court judgment in a business interruption test case, not all BI policies were covered by the judgment. Sadly, most SMEs found that they were not covered on their policies as the cover was focused on property damage.

IT and GDPR
Ensuring adequate backup facilities and regularly checking they work is a priority. Consider access codes and passwords too. A

fully backed-up system is not a great deal of help if no one can access it. Directors and key personnel should have a hard copy of the business continuity plan at alternative premises, and it may be advisable to lodge a copy with the company accountants or solicitors.

It is virtually impossible to operate a business nowadays without fully functioning IT systems and, in most cases, a company website. But such systems also bring their own challenges in terms of internal and external security.

As well as back-ups, it is essential to ensure appropriate security systems are in place. It is probably advisable to speak to an IT consultant specialising in this area to get the most suitable system for your business to protect your website and the data you hold on all devices.

As well as the internal need to protect data, it is also a legal requirement to ensure the security of any third-party personal data held. This could be employees, customers, members, or any other **personal** data you hold. Data protection under the General Data Protection Regulation (GDPR) applies to most UK businesses and organisations. They must be registered with the Information Commissioner's Office (ICO) and meet statutory ICO codes of practice.

GDPR also affects websites, and companies should ensure compliance. A few of the requirements:

- Forms that invite users to subscribe should be blank or default to 'no';
- Privacy Notice and Terms and Conditions;
- Cookie banner and statement.

The above is only a brief outline of GDPR requirements. You may require a consultant to help ensure you are compliant.

Another aspect of your business that most start-ups and small businesses ignore is protecting any intellectual property assets such as:

- The names of your products or brands
- Your inventions
- The design or look of your products
- Things you write, make or produce

Copyright, patents, designs and trademarks are all types of intellectual property protection (IPP).

If someone copied or stole your intellectual property, would it have a material impact on your business? If it would, you would be well advised to seek a specialist and ensure appropriate IPP is in place.

As I have previously mentioned, most small business owners do not have the skill sets or capacity to manage all aspects of business operations adequately; therefore, delegation or outsourcing is necessary. That does not mean completely relinquishing control. Similarly, it does not mean micromanaging every aspect of your business.

For example, if you do not manage the accounting records yourself, do you receive regular understandable financial information? How do you ensure all financial and legal reporting responsibilities are efficiently carried out? How do you ensure all other legal obligations are being met?

It Really Is Just Good Business

Operating efficiently and profitably, and caring about people and the environment, are NOT mutually exclusive. Taking a sustainable, holistic approach to business means looking at all aspects of operations in tandem. It's a strategy that really is just good business.

Unquestionably, being a micro or small business owner can be extremely challenging, but it can also be immensely rewarding, especially if you are committed to making a positive contribution to society. As environmentalist Dame Jane Goodall says:

What you do makes a difference, and you have to decide what kind of difference you want to make.

If you follow the points made in this book, aim to make a positive contribution to society, and have sound systems in place, you'll love what you do even more. And as Steve Jobs says:

Your work will fill a large part of your life, and the only way to be truly satisfied is to do what you believe is great work. The only way to do great work is to love what you do.

And as a bonus, profits will follow. Because, as I may have mentioned before:

* * *

DOING GOOD IS GOOD FOR BUSINESS

What's Next?

What's Next For You?

The purpose of this book is to encourage and inspire a different way of doing business. I hope it has proved thought provoking. I hope it does inspire an approach to business that feeds your soul; that's good for your people, your community and society in general; that's good for our fragile environment. And that as a natural progression of thinking and working differently, you will have a sustainable and more profitable business model, and a business that is an integral part of a jigsaw that is slowly coming together to make the world a better place for us and future generations. And last, but not least, a business that makes you both proud and happy.

At whatever stage you are at on your journey and with your business, a future business, or any organisations you are involved with in any way whatsoever, I hope with all my heart this has inspired you to start making those changes, remembering that all those baby steps each small business takes cumulatively have a mammoth impact.

To know that has happened, that I have inspired you even just a tiny little bit, will really make my heart sing. Do please drop me an email and let me know.

And if I may ask at this point, a review on Amazon would be much appreciated because good reviews will encourage more people to read this book and, as a result, encourage more people to embrace a responsible business approach.

I hope you will also consider applying for membership of ORB because while individually we need to commit to establishing, acting upon, and communicating our values internally and externally, being part of a movement for a better way of doing business can elevate the speed of change to an enhanced level. We must strive together to make responsible business the norm. I urge you to join us and help to change the world, one small business at a time, and to realise our vision of thriving, vibrant cities, towns and villages, where small businesses play a vital role in their local communities, contributing to social, environmental, and economic sustainability, and setting an example of ethical and responsible business behaviour in the UK and across the world.

And why not also consider the robust, evidenced-based Responsible Business Standard certification if you want to elevate your reputation to an even higher level?

Because as sole proprietors, freelancers, and micro and small business owners, you have the power to change the world – one small business at a time. But do remember, it isn't enough just to be doing the right things; you need to authentically communicate your purpose and values internally and externally as loudly as you possibly can.

What's Next for Me?
My Birthday Legacy Gift

In May 2022, ORB was proud to win the Corporate LiveWire's Community Interest Company of the Year Award for Innovation and Excellence. The award bears testament to the team's commitment, hard work and achievements since we launched in 2010.

The irony is that ORB relinquished its CIC status within three months of receiving this award. Why? Primarily because ORB was a CIC limited by shares and I did not feel this was appropriate for the organisation.

We had already been approached a few times to sell ORB, and it was abundantly obvious in each case that the intent was to use the reputation we had established and the various platforms we had developed to expand into a different, more lucrative marketplace. One that did not prioritise supporting micro and small businesses. One that would look to working with much bigger companies because, without question, that is a far easier way to maximise income potential.

I wanted to protect ORB for the future. I wanted to guarantee it could not be sold. I wanted to ensure that ORB always focused on driving the movement for a better way of doing business within the small business community.

And so, on 30 August 2022, on my seventy-second birthday, Mike and I gifted ORB to our members. To facilitate the process, ORB simultaneously merged into a new company with a different structure, thus ensuring all current and future members of ORB jointly own the new company. (This is a common structure for not-for-profit membership organisations, with members legally known as guarantors.)

I am incredibly proud that the National Organisation for Responsible Micro, Small and Medium-sized Businesses has been established as a Company Limited by Guarantee with a board of directors to oversee the management of the company and a Member Council that can elect up to three directors to the board to ensure the views of its members are always represented at board level.

And yes, The National Organisation for Responsible Micro, Small and Medium-sized Businesses is quite a mouthful. The new company will continue to trade as the Organisation for Responsible Businesses, abbreviated to ORB as appropriate. So, from an external perspective, nothing will have changed. Our vision and mission, the logo, the websites, the membership processes, all our courses, the Responsible Business Standard Certification, etc., will all remain the same, subject to 'normal' future developments.

And yet this change is incredibly significant.

The purpose and fundamental processes and procedures of ORB are all detailed in the new company's Articles of Association. As enshrined in law by the Companies Act 2006, the Articles can only be changed by a Special Resolution which can only be passed if approved by a majority of not less than 75 per cent of votes cast by those entitled to vote. All members shall have the right to vote on Special Resolutions.

Our legacy gift has protected the future of the company. It has protected its purpose.

What was initially launched without specific altruistic intent became precisely that: a passion for making a difference that transcended the desire for personal financial gain. At the time of writing, neither Mike nor I have taken any income from the company, either as salary or dividends.

What do these changes mean for me?

Mike and I are in our seventies now. Mike has semi-retired, but I am still firmly in the driving seat of ORB. I am not ready to retire yet and cannot imagine ever fully doing so. Nonetheless, I recognise that it is time to start handing over the reins to a new team with the energy and inspiration to take this national organisation to the next level. Protecting the company as above is a huge part of my exit strategy.

I am excited by the changes that will undoubtedly happen over the next few years. I am also looking forward to having more free time, yet equally hoping that I will be speaking at more events across the country and meeting wonderful people committed to responsible business practices. Do come and say hello if you see me at an event and have read this book, are a member of ORB, or would just like to chat about all things responsible business.

* * *

Rather than writing detailed information about the Organisation for Responsible Businesses, I urge you to check out our websites, connect with me on LinkedIn, or send me an email:

Main membership website: https://orbuk.org.uk
Directory of Members: https://
theresponsiblebusinessdirectory.co.uk
Responsible Business Standard: https://
responsiblebusinessstandard.org.uk
LinkedIn personal: https://www.linkedin.com/in/jillpoet/
LinkedIn ORB: https://www.linkedin.com/company/
organisation-for-responsible-businesses
Email: jill@jillpoet.co.uk

Resources

Membership Organisations

I recommend that all small businesses have membership in at least one major small business membership organisation or a relevant trade association.

The national membership organisations detailed below provide a great deal of support and information, with regular updates advising on any changes in legislation. Membership of the first four organisations mentioned includes 24-hour legal advice helplines and specific cover for potentially challenging and unexpected events such as HMRC investigations.

Rates and benefits vary, and offerings change, so please compare and ask other small business owners to share their experiences.

FSB

https://www.fsb.org.uk

National Federation of Self-Employed & Small Businesses Ltd

FPB

https://www.fpb.org/

Forum of Private Business Ltd

British Chambers of Commerce

https://www.britishchambers.org.uk

There are various Chambers of Commerce across the UK, all accredited by The British Chambers of Commerce. To become a member, you must join a local accredited chamber. You can find a list using this link: https://www.britishchambers.org.uk/page/join-a-chamber.

IOD

https://www.iod.com/

Institute of Directors

CBI

https://www.cbi.org.uk

Confederation of British Industry

Enterprise Nation

https://www.enterprisenation.com

Enterprise Nation operates on a different basis. It is currently free to join and is particularly useful for start-ups and small businesses. Although it doesn't provide the same level of protection as the above organisations, it does offer a range of excellent resources, including the Start-Up Hub.

* * *

Organisations Providing Support & Guidance

Below are details of government and non-departmental public bodies that provide help and guidance to help ensure you meet legislation and best practice.

Additionally, ad hoc programmes and grants are frequently available in different regions of the UK to support small businesses. Your local authority, which you can find using the following link, may be able to provide information, particularly if they have an economic development team: https://www.gov. uk/find-local-council.

ACAS

https://www.acas.org.uk

The Advisory Conciliation and Arbitration Service (ACAS) gives employees and employers free, impartial advice on workplace rights, rules and best practices. ACAS offers a range of tools and resources, including free templates for letters, forms and policy documents; training options including free e-learning modules and webinars for employers and employees on a wide range of employment issues; and a dispute resolution service.

You can also subscribe for email updates on employment legislation changes, HR guidance and tips, and research and events information.

HSE

https://www.hse.gov.uk

The Health and Safety Executive (HSE) is the independent regulator for work-related health, safety and illness. The website contains a range of help and advice, including various templates, The Health and Safety Toolbox, various free downloads, books and more.

It is worth subscribing to free email updates that cover a wide range of health and safety topics and industries.

The HSE has a wide range of powers but nowadays prefers to adopt a supportive and advisory approach.

While HSE is responsible for enforcing health and safety at certain workplaces, some premises come under the jurisdiction of the local authority environmental health department.

The link below clarifies which authority you should contact according to your query.

https://www.hse.gov.uk/contact/authority.htm

DVSA

https://www.gov.uk/government/organisations/driver-and-vehicle-standards-agency

The Driver and Vehicle Standards Agency (DVSA) provides a full range of information relating to licensing, testing and enforcement services with the aim of improving the road worthiness standards of vehicles and ensuring compliance of operators and drivers.

The Pensions Regulator (TPR)

https://www.thepensionsregulator.gov.uk
The Pensions Regulator protects the UK's workplace pensions by ensuring employers, business advisors, trustees, and pension specialists can fulfil their duties to scheme members.

If you are considering taking on an employee or are just about to employ someone for the first time, the TPR provides a quick online process to help you understand your legal liabilities and work out what you need to do.

https://www.thepensionsregulator.gov.uk/en/employers/new-employers

GOV.UK

https://www.gov.uk/browse/business
The GOV.UK website contains comprehensive information on a range of business topics, including employing staff for the first time. Links to more authoritative websites are often included. This is usually a good starting point if you need business information and do not know where to look.

Equality and Human Rights Commission

https://www.equalityhumanrights.com/en/advice-and-guidance
The Equality and Human Rights Commission promotes equality and human rights to create a fairer Britain. They do this by providing advice and guidance, working to implement an effective legislative framework, and raising awareness of people's rights. The website offers comprehensive information for organisations relating to equal pay, equality law and discrimination.

Living Wage Foundation

https://www.livingwage.org.uk/

The Foundation believes that a hard day's work deserves a fair day's pay, based on the cost of living, not just the government minimum. Visit the website if you would like to ensure you pay the Living Wage and perhaps become accredited as a Living Wage Employer.

The Carbon Trust

https://www.carbontrust.com

The Carbon Trust advises businesses, governments and the public sector on strategy, risks and opportunities, target-setting, carbon reduction plans and transitioning to a low carbon world. The website includes a range of information and resources, including Steps to Energy Saving: Tools for SMEs, which is particularly useful as it includes the following:

https://www.carbontrust.com/resources/steps-to-energy-saving-tools-for-smes

- Carbon Footprint Calculator
- SME Energy Benchmark Tool
- Lighting Business Case Tool
- Fleet Upgrade Tool

Supply Chain Sustainability School

https://www.supplychainschool.co.uk

The school is an excellent FREE online resource for those working in construction, facilities management, homes and infrastructure sectors in England, Scotland and Wales.

Learning options are provided at beginner, intermediate and advanced levels and include:

- E-learning modules

- Videos
- Documents and Presentations
- Training Events and Workshops
- Toolkits
- Case Studies

WRAP

https://wrap.org.uk

WRAP (Waste Resources Action Programme) is a UK-based charity that works internationally to help reduce waste by changing how things are produced, consumed and disposed of. It focuses on four key areas: food and drink, plastic packaging, clothing and textiles, collections and recycling. You can register for the sector-specific business briefing newsletter if you work in any of these areas.

There are various guides, tools and case studies available on the website.

Environment Agency

https://www.gov.uk/government/organisations/environment-agency

The Environment Agency in England is responsible for:

- regulating major industry and waste
- treatment of contaminated land
- water quality and resources
- fisheries
- inland river, estuary and harbour navigations
- conservation and ecology
- managing the risk of flooding from main rivers, reservoirs, estuaries and the sea.

Find out and apply for environmental permits, waste permits and licences, and report any environmental incidents via the website.

Ellen Macarthur Foundation

https://ellenmacarthurfoundation.org/

The Ellen Macarthur Foundation is a registered charity focusing on the circular economy. The website includes a range of resources plus membership and newsletter options.

Business Companion

https://www.businesscompanion.info

Business Companion covers trading standards and consumer protection legislation in England, Scotland and Wales. The site provides free, impartial, legal guidance for businesses with a comprehensive range of quick and comprehensive guides. There is also a 'Get Started' option for small businesses and start-ups.

Work for Good Ltd

https://workforgood.co.uk/

Work for Good is a private company limited by shares registered with the Fundraising Regulator.

Registering on the WfG platform enables small businesses to quickly set up Commercial Participation Agreements and marketing campaigns for charities of their choice. Charities must be UK registered, but they may have specific projects anywhere in the world.

B1G1

https://b1g1.com

B1G1 (Buy1Give1 Pte Ltd) is run by a social enterprise (registered company in Singapore) and non-profit organization (501(c)3 registered in the US).

B1G1 operates internally, providing a platform for businesses to support small projects across the globe by linking a regular business activity to a micro impact. For example, perhaps for every xxx you sell, you provide ten days of access to clean water to families in Ethiopia.

NVCO

https://www.ncvo.org.uk/ncvo-volunteering/find-a-volunteer-centre

The National Council for Voluntary Organisations (NVCO) represents and supports its affiliated local voluntary organisation members across England. These local organisations, in turn, support thousands of charities, community groups and social enterprises. If you want to engage with the local community and support charities, community groups or mentoring projects and don't know how to get started, your local VCO (Voluntary Community Organisation) or your local authority may be able to signpost you accordingly.

SEDEX

https://www.sedex.com

Sedex (Sedex Information Exchange Ltd) is a trade membership organisation working with businesses to improve working conditions in global supply chains. If you have an extensive overseas supply chain, SEDEX can provide supply chain visibility, audits and assessments.

ICO

https://ico.org.uk/

The ICO (Information Commissioners Office) is the UK's independent authority set up to uphold information rights in the public interest, promoting openness by public bodies and data privacy for individuals.

As well as enabling you to register your company under the UK GDPR (General Data Protection Regulation,) the website provides a host of information and resources.

OSBC

https://www.smallbusinesscommissioner.gov.uk

The Office of the Small Business Commissioner was set up in 2016 to tackle late payment and unfavourable payment practices in the private sector.

The OSBC considers complaints from small businesses about payment problems they have with their larger business customers, providing support and advice and making non-binding recommendations, as appropriate, on how the parties should resolve their disputes.

You can also register your commitment to prompt payment by becoming a signatory to the Prompt Payment Code. https://www.smallbusinesscommissioner.gov.uk/ppc/signatory-details/

HMRC

I don't doubt you know HMRC is responsible for collecting taxes. However, you may not know that HMRC provides a valuable help and support mail service. Add your email address via the link below then you'll be given the option to choose the subjects you would like regular updates on.
https://subscriptions.hmrc.gov.uk/

BUSINESS
BOOKS

Business Books

Business Books publishes practical guides
and insightful non-fiction for beginners and professionals.
Covering aspects from management skills, leadership and
organizational change to positive work environments, career
coaching and self-care for managers, our books are a valuable
addition to those working in the world of business.

15 Ways to Own Your Future
Take Control of Your Destiny in Business and in Life
Michael Khouri
A 15-point blueprint for creating better collaboration, enjoyment,
and success in business and in life.
Paperback: 978-1-78535-300-0 ebook: 978-1-78535-301-7

The Common Excuses of the Comfortable Compromiser
Understanding Why People Oppose Your Great Idea
Matt Crossman
Comfortable compromisers block the way of anyone trying to
change anything. This is your guide to their common excuses.
Paperback: 978-1-78099-595-3 ebook: 978-1-78099-596-0

The Failing Logic of Money
Duane Mullin
Money is wasteful and cruel, causes war, crime and dysfunctional
feudalism. Humankind needs happiness, peace and abundance. So
banish money and use technology and knowledge to rid the world
of war, crime and poverty.
Paperback: 978-1-84694-259-4 ebook: 978-1-84694-888-6

Mastering the Mommy Track
Juggling Career and Kids in Uncertain Times
Erin Flynn Jay
Mastering the Mommy Track tells the stories of everyday working
mothers, the challenges they have faced, and lessons learned.
Paperback: 978-1-78099-123-8 ebook: 978-1-78099-124-5

Readers of ebooks can buy or view any of these bestsellers by clicking on the live link in the title. Most titles are published in paperback and as an ebook. Paperbacks are available in traditional bookshops. Both print and ebook formats are available online.

Find more titles and sign up to our readers' newsletter at http://www.jhpbusiness-books.com/

Facebook: https://www.facebook.com/JHPNonFiction/

Twitter: @JHPNonFiction